AT HOME ANYWHERE

FEEL AT HOME
WHEREVER LIFE TAKES YOU

At home anywhere

RACHAEL LYNN

—

FEEL AT HOME
WHEREVER LIFE TAKES YOU

This edition was published by The Dreamwork Collective

The Dreamwork Collective LLC, Dubai, United Arab Emirates

thedreamworkcollective.com

Printed and bound in the United Arab Emirates

Cover Design: Myriam Arab

ISBN 9789948364665

Approved by National Media Council

Dubai, United Arab Emirates

MC-02-01-3294563

Printed and bound in the United Arab Emirates

by Al Ghurair Printing and Publishing LLC

For my family,

for supporting every inkling, desire, and emotion within me. You have given me wings.

For anyone wondering if there's something wrong with them because of who they are and how they feel things.

All of you keep me going.

Dear life,

Thank you for sending me on this magnificent journey.
I am far from home, but I know my real home is with you,
wherever that may physically take me.

Thank you for allowing me to see all of the magic you've
created through the people I meet, the places I go,
the languages I hear, and the food I eat.

May I always remember my purpose—
to experience and feel the full depth of living,
and remember that my way is not the only way.

Thank you for guiding me and loving me fully,
for returning me to myself,
and for bringing me home,
over and over again.

Contents

*My favorite
line of work is
learning
how to love
myself harder.*

Setting the Foundation

Fourteen times. By the age of thirty, I'd moved to a new house or apartment fourteen times. Many of those moves happened within Buffalo, New York, where I grew up and spent the first twenty-three years of my life. But it wasn't until the farthest and most recent move—from Toronto, Canada, to Dubai in the United Arab Emirates—that I started to see moving as a defining thread in my life.

In the past, I measured myself by my relationships and career changes. Those were the areas I believed my worth was drawn from. Was I in a relationship? Often, yes. Was it a good one? Often, no. And was I making money? Was it by doing something I enjoyed? This question always made me hesitate. I had jobs I was good at and valued for, but I felt like I was wasting my time and that I was missing a bigger purpose.

After leaving a long-term relationship and my last corporate job in Manhattan in 2013, I was finally listening to my heart when it came to what it really took for me to be happy. But I was also lost. Now what do I define my own value by? How do I have the relationship I've always wanted? And how do I create a working environment that doesn't feel like work? I envied the people who claimed they had it all. As much as I wasn't sure if that life was real, I wanted to try and create my version of it anyway.

Luckily, I grew up around parents who dabbled in the personal development and self-help industry. We also weren't averse to going to therapy or talking to counselors. Throughout my childhood, my mom would play inspirational, more spiritually leaning tapes—in the house, in the car, and anywhere she possibly could. As a teenager, I found this practice suitably annoying and refused to pay attention. My dad, on the other hand, had a real flair for business and finance, and he often ended up sounding like a motivational speaker. For him, good habits, mental discipline and hard work were the cornerstones of success. This I also ignored for a while. Having these ideas float around me my whole life might have motivated me subconsciously, but I didn't consider their value until this new identity-crisis point in my early twenties. I wondered to myself, why did my family have all this information around us, and yet I was still feeling totally clueless? Didn't I know by now that my thoughts created my reality, that I just had to discipline myself and "want it bad enough" or have faith? I decided that if I was going to make any kind of change, I had to take it a step further. What did that mean for twenty-four-year-old me? I did what any financially savvy young person on a New York City budget would do: I handed my trusty credit card over to my very first life coach and maxed it out on the first payment.

A quick aside: mentioning life coaches can cause people to roll their eyes, as they imagine vegan gatherings, drum circles, or a walk over hot coal. I've attended two out of those three things—I'll let you guess which. . . .

In my experience, a good life coach is trained in supporting you to achieve a certain goal and mixes action-based work with emotional-based work. They often do this by creating a plan of specific actions for you to take to reach your goal, coupled with an in-depth look at the beliefs and thought processes that might've been stopping you from taking those actions on your own. Working with a coach can range from identifying trauma from your childhood that's holding you back to creating a healthy lifestyle and identifying the reasons you emotionally sabotage your diets. Having used counseling, therapy, and now coaching at different stages of my life, coaching has been the place where I felt my actions were actually changing and I wasn't just gathering a logical understanding of what was causing my problems. If you need support to function normally in life, I suggest working with a clinical professional like a psychologist first. If you want to make improvements in your life to further benefit your experience, go with a coach. This is only my personal opinion; you must do what's best for you.

Getting back to the twenty-four-year-old NYC me, I felt like I'd tried it all, and just going to therapy and reading books weren't cutting it. Maxing out my credit card was a risk I thought I had to take when I couldn't stand repeating my mistakes anymore. I wanted someone to hold me accountable to what I said I wanted and who I wanted to be. Within months of hiring my first coach, I got so enveloped in the personal-development world that I started working in it myself—editing other coaches' courses and books, becoming an assistant coach, and helping them run their businesses. Not only did I learn how coaches do what they do and how it impacted my own life, but I got to see how other people were changing their lives too. And my life really did change.

Over five years of having support, practicing self-reflection, and being single helped more pieces of my life come together. I got to know who I was without the roles I had taken on: the giving one, the mature one, the strong one, the smart one, and the kind of bratty, independent one. I learned why I allowed myself to be and stay in relationships that were unhealthy and noncommittal, and how to be more honest with who I was in the world. Doing so gave me tools to fall back on when I was depressed about my move to Dubai and new identity as a wife.

Though I no longer work for coaches now, I still hire them

when I want them. In fact, my last coach, Amanda, officiated my wedding. Having support in my life continues to break open everything I thought I knew about who I was and allows for a version of myself I thought was reserved for women born into different lives or circumstances.

Within the pages of this book, you'll hear of some lessons I gleaned from the coaches in my life. There are personal stories both before my move to Dubai and during. I will share with you the story of finally being with my husband, a man whom I had essentially rejected ten years prior to our wedding because he was "too good for me." He is the man who led me on my journey to the desert and the journey to creating this book. I will share with you the awkward and painful pieces of moving transition that stuck out most to me, and the tools I've gathered along the way to help get through them.

Keep This One Thing in Mind

What I deeply want for you to hear before you go further is that there is no award for the fastest completion of the exercises in these pages. There is no quiz at the end to see if you are "over" your grief or your discomfort from your move. Because you won't be over it—not with the first reading, and not unless you're also listening to yourself.

I also ask you to commit to being here for yourself through thick and thin, and to love yourself when you're a mess—*especially* when you're a mess. Because you're not going to get it right all the time. There are still some days where I wonder how long we'll be in Dubai and how hard it will when we move again. I will need my own book then just like you need it now. That's the truth and it's okay. It's time to stop trying to be perfect.

Throughout the writing and editing of this book, I traveled and visited family. Family came to visit me. New friends moved away. And what that taught me was that in fact, the grief and discomfort actually never end. There is always a new transition that appears, and that's the life we've signed up for. For so long I believed that if I just hired the right coach or read the right book everything would be right in my life and I would never experience sadness, fear, or anxiety again. I want us to let ourselves off that hook together. My coaches didn't fix my life, but they guided me to do it myself. When I didn't listen to them, nothing changed, and I still had to pay the invoice. This book will not save you from yourself or from some struggles, but it will help you get to know yourself better. To be a better friend to yourself when you need it most. Trust that there's even just a little information here to help you. We're here in it together. I'm grateful you've decided to read about my version of the experience of moving across the world.

A disclaimer: There are women all over the world who have moved more times than I have, who have moved to more challenging places—remote places where they can't speak the language or places that put their families at risk. There are women who have gone through the trials of losing a family member when living far away, and of birthing, schooling, and homeschooling their children. Those have not been my experiences and I can't claim them to be. I am writing from a white-privileged, able-bodied, passport-privileged, financially privileged, pre-motherhood place. Really, I've got it easy. The depths of my transition may not compare to yours in the same ways. That's the truth of it, and I also know that some of the activities we go through in this book together can still support you. Our foundations are the same—we have transitioned and we feel alone. I believe so deeply in my core that connection with ourselves and the right community will get us through anything. I hope that I'm right, and I hope that you're open to hearing what's meant for you.

So let's begin.

Walking toward the future is much better than running away from the past.

CHAPTER 1

Searching for Home

Growing up in Buffalo, there are two homes in particular that I have the strongest memories of. The first was a home of play, chicken pox, an attempt at running away, and Halloween costumes. There were not-so-fun family times, but it was where I felt most like a kid. The second home was my grandparents' place, where we lived with both of my maternal grandparents and my aunt Linda for many years. There are memories of fullness in these places, of family and laughter and being annoyed by the people you love.

My parents divorced when I was a baby, so I often visited Canada, where my father and his family lived. That family was always where deep talks around the dining table occurred. Staying with my dad on weekends and holiday visits, just the two of us, meant Saturday morning cartoons and adventures. With all of those memories tucked away, I have no memories of home being a place I stayed for longer than three or four years. It was never a place where my entire family was. I hadn't realized how that shifting affected me until I got to Dubai. It makes my heart swell thinking of military families, foster children, refugees, and all those forced to leave home, uncertain about where they'll go next. How lucky we are to experience a move abroad or cross-country, mostly out of choice. And still as the privileged ones, we find these transitions so challenging.

My moves were "micro" at first—same city, different apartment. But once I graduated from University in Buffalo, the distances grew. For most of my twenties, I envisioned a life traveling the world. This imaginary life involved having homes in various countries and supporting myself through a nomadic laptop lifestyle it seemed everyone online had: a lifestyle where everything I wanted to do could be done where I had a Wi-Fi signal, and I was unattached to a physical location. I would travel the world, hopping from café to coworking space to hotel lobby, making friends along the way. This vision I had wasn't concerned with "reality"—about what life would feel like never being close to my family, how lonely it would feel when I had more than two days without plans, or what would happen when I fell in love, got married, and craved nesting and stability.

That's what daydreaming youth is for, I suppose. And it inspired my first big move at twenty-three to New York City. Sunnyside, Queens, to be specific. This family-oriented little neighborhood off the 7 train would be the farthest distance anyone in my family had ever moved to. It was an hour plane ride away. This was a big deal for them, but I didn't have the time to think about that. I was ready to go and take on the adventure that was the city everyone dreams of being in. It would be the place where everything in life would come together and I'd be the adult I always wanted to be. In retrospect, I wanted to run away from all the mess that I felt surrounded me in Buffalo—those poor dating decisions, an unfulfilling career, and the grief I felt after losing many people I loved very close together. In my mind, the city of dreams would solve all that.

New York City gave me exactly what I needed. I think it does that for everyone. But the concrete jungle didn't give me a perfect life. It was a kick in the butt to realize that even though I was in a new place, my feelings and the things happening in my life hadn't changed much at all. New York City was that place I mentioned earlier where I started to get more curious about why nothing felt all that different. Why I seemed to be making choices I didn't really want to make.

Two years later at twenty-six, freshly single and knee-deep in looking at my thoughts and behavioral patterns with my life coaches, I had to get out of the city. The lease was coming up on the apartment I shared with my best friend (who happened to be from Bahrain, a tiny country close to Dubai), and I took that as the opportunity not to renew. I was still searching for something when I made that decision: a feeling that I thought would feel better than any feeling I'd ever had before—a feeling of home.

For many years, home was a feeling other people had. When they could return to a place where their parents would both be, where their childhood room was untouched, and where they lived until they got married. And then lived happily ever after in their new home, with their partners and their children who continued the cycle. Home was the ability to breathe a sigh of relief when you walk in the front door. It was the white-picket-fence story that many people want and nobody has when you peer into the back of the dusty kitchen cabinets.

This idea of Home hung a carrot over my head, taunting, *I'm here. This is the place you're meant to be. I'm perfectly, magnificently, content. Everything is always great here. Come find me.*

I left New York without a real plan for where to go next. I was starting to trust myself more and had to hold on to faith that everything would somehow work out. I was finally listening to my gut, so it had to, right? With little income and an even tinier plan, I stayed with family, rented Airbnbs in Canada, and borrowed couches in West Palm Beach, Florida. I even ended the whole thing with a solo trip to California for Wanderlust Festival, a festival filled with yoga and inspirational talks, complete with blue highlights in my hair. I was really going all out on my newly discovered free spirit.

With no clear home in sight, my soul-searching led me back to the best place I could afford—which also happened to be the exact place I tried to get away from. Buffalo. Except this time, a different kind of maturing and forgiveness had taken place. There were places in Buffalo that held memories that I had wanted to avoid for so long. But upon my return it was clear that I was different now, and Buffalo was too.

After about ten months there, I was feeling more spiritually solid than ever. In discovering the art museums, new restaurants, and cafés, I saw that my "Queen City," as it's been coined, was having its renaissance. My creativity was blooming, but something was missing. I was still treading water. I felt like I finally loved myself and my work, but I was still incredibly impatient about when my future husband would arrive in the picture.

And that's when the itch came back . . .

There's got to be more out there for me than this.
I'm going to make something of myself. I don't think it's here.
You've always loved Canada, try Canada.
But should I? This is getting exhausting.
Why can't I just figure it out?
I'll know when I know.

I'll know when I know. I've always told myself this—mostly about meeting the right man, but also about life. I had done so much research and work on intuition, connecting with myself, and trusting myself. So when the itch came back, I began to pay attention.

The knowing of your intuition brings a feeling of peace, followed by a little bit of excitement. You feel all that, just seconds before your mind has a chance to chime in with all of its thoughts about why it's a terrible idea. When you know, you know softly in your heart, not loudly in your head.

—

As I now considered myself a seasoned gut checker, I got my butt in the car and drove to Toronto, the major Canadian city two hours from Buffalo, to see if my feelings were correct. And as the city skyline arrived to greet me from the Queen Elizabeth Way highway one late summer afternoon in 2016, a few tears started to roll down my cheeks.

Tears indicated the quiet feeling of relief. Of knowing. And just like that, I knew. Toronto would be the next place I lived. Would this be the place I actually found Home?

It was my first time living without family or roommates. My first real time on my own. I had family about forty-five minutes from the city, which was just close enough to make me feel settled, but no friends. I was working remotely from my apartment and cafés. I'd achieved a long-held dream of having freedom from a corporate office, but that still meant I had to find friends somewhere.

Fast-forward to three months of living in that beautiful Canadian city, and I was overbooked with things to do. I went on such a rampage of making sure I was going to meet people that I eventually had to take a break from all the socializing. I remember a new friend saying to me, "When did you move here, a few years ago?" They were shocked at how integrated I was in the community in such a short amount of time. The combination of living alone, single life (the longest I had been single since high school), and all of the inner work was finally paying off. I felt more connected to myself and a community than ever before.

I figured I would be in Toronto for many years, if not forever. But little did I know life had other plans. The happiness and connection with myself I had created led me to a realization that I was in love with a man I'd met nine years before, in university.

The catch? He lived in Dubai.

Am I Really Moving Again?

I remember so clearly the day my now-husband and I started talking over a WhatsApp call about what we would do if we really wanted to "do this," aka get married. Almost thirty now, I was still 100 percent location independent workwise. He had responsibilities in the Middle East, so the easiest decision also felt hard. "I'm happy in Toronto. I feel like I have a real home here," I said through a few tears.

I had never felt at home about a place before! I had never felt a pull to stay where I was, a desire to expand my presence into every nook of the city I could find. I had found that feeling of home I was searching for, and I didn't recognize it until it was time to leave.

I was a bit shocked by this realization, because getting to a place where I could feel like I loved my life and where I was took a lot of time. I had worked so hard to create that community in Canada, to make friends, and do my best to take care of myself. Was I going to give all that up now that I finally felt good? And for a split-second, an overprotective narrative asked, *Was I really going to switch up my current happiness for a man?*

But those thoughts passed quickly. Being with him was another intuitive knowing, and I'd regret it if I didn't listen. I knew, because this time being with this man and moving to Dubai wasn't me running away from anything. It wasn't like that first move away from Buffalo to New York City. Or from Buffalo to Toronto. For once, I loved my life, my friends, and the way my relationships with my family were growing. I loved everything in Toronto, except the never-ending months of snow. No, I wasn't running from anything. Running away from discomfort and stepping purposefully into something you're meant for are two very different things. This time, I was walking toward something important. My husband, our relationship, and my life. I could feel it.

It was the next right step to take. It just was a 6,875-mile bigger step than I expected.

And what I've come to know for sure is that I needed that distance to wake me up. Marriage and moving were two shocks to my system, and they were also amazing gifts. They sent me into an identity crisis I could have never foreseen. An identity crisis is a huge part of a moving transition, and I wasn't prepared for a double whammy. Who was I now that I was a wife? Who was I now I'd been catapulted into a lifestyle totally different than the one I grew up in?

The Journey of Transition

Most people probably do a lot of research before moving to a new place. I certainly did. But if I could do it over again, I would've spent less time looking into where to eat in Dubai and more time learning how to support myself emotionally through the transition. I thought my self-care practices, the love between my husband and I, and my luck making deep friendships in Toronto would be all I needed to replicate success.

I'm a queen of list-making. I've made lists of all the lists I have to make and when to make them. When we were getting ready for Dubai, I made lists of the government offices I had to visit, the things I wanted to pack, give away, and sell. I listed out all the things I needed to buy in North America that I wasn't sure I could find once we got there. What supplements and snacks were best for me on the thirteen-hour flight and how to nourish my skin from the lack of hydration. Luckily there are endless blogs and YouTube videos on doing all that.

But I hadn't prepared my lists and watched the videos for the things that would support me once I got over the excitement of unpacking and real-life routine settled in. It probably would've been easier if I had just asked my husband if we could keep traveling forever and never really land. At least it would have delayed the feelings.

I didn't falter for long. In the grand scheme of things, it was about nine months of hard adjustment, and then the occasional set back here and there. But I can be impatient. I was worried that in my depression, I was missing out on a beautiful opportunity to experience what life was offering me. Perhaps the worst part about not feeling like yourself is knowing you could feel better, but you can't seem to shake it. We beat ourselves up for beating ourselves up.

It wasn't until I was in the depths of my low, which I explain fully later on, that I began to research how people cope with major moves and with change in general. As of 2019, there are an overwhelming number of people sharing versions of their experience, including academic research behind the subject of moving abroad. Corporate relocation agencies are everywhere. Which is a good sign. People want to help us and share their experiences. Turns out, that as with most things in life, we're no special snowflakes when it comes to moving transitions and feeling stuck!

I definitely recognized how the accounts I found reflected my experience and felt some relief knowing I wasn't alone. But many of the solutions to relocation anxiety and depression seemed sterile. I was craving more. I couldn't fully relate to the accounts of women moving with their husbands and staying home with the kids to homeschool. I didn't relate to the expats who were documenting their dinners and nights out. Traveling all over the world without a real home base, as many people are now doing, also wasn't my thing. Where was someone like me? I was a young, newly married woman with a desire to create something meaningful in the world through my work—interested in self-reflection, wellness, and personal development. There had to be a blend somewhere! But I got impatient, and decided to create a solution of #allthethings that could work to help me feel like myself again.

Throughout this book, I've included the truth of my own experience, the things that helped me and the things I wish I had done in hindsight. I tried using the tools I learned from working in personal development and I read all about the different stages of relocation anxiety that many experts had outlined. In this book, I'll walk you through the key stages: the Decision to Move, Saying Goodbye, New Beginnings, Acting Fine, the Moment It Hits You, Your Low Point, Identity Formation, and—finally—Thriving. Wherever you are on this path, it's still worth spending time on the phases you think you might have already passed through. Pay attention to the experience you went through and give yourself a chance to take some credit for everything. Don't skip ahead if it seems too simple. Profound change often happens in the places we forget to look or write off because it seems easy. I don't want you to miss out on why you're taking the journey in the first place—the journey to the home inside of you.

If You Learned Only This

- The stages of transition and change have been studied for years now. Formal studies around international living are also taking place. You are not alone in the things you're experiencing. In fact, you're normal!

- Be your own best friend throughout this journey and throughout this book. The book can't save you, but your dedication to yourself can.

- Come back to this book and the practices as many times and as often as you need. There is no final destination to rush toward, though I know how desperately you want to feel you have it all together.

- We are going through this together. You're not alone.

Write It Out

1. This first section is simply about awareness of yourself. What's happening for you right now? Put a word to the feeling you're experiencing when you think about your move.

2. What stage of your moving transition do you think you're in? Journal out your thoughts and examine if there is any phase you might have skipped over.

Thoughts to Help You

Say Them as Often as You Need.

- I am open to allowing whatever feelings I need to feel during this time.

- I am really proud of myself for taking this big, scary risk of moving.

- I will give myself more time than I think I need to adjust to all of this change.

- There is no finish line. I am right on time.

- I've figured out many things, so I can figure this out too.

Sometimes, you get everything you want—it just doesn't fall into place the way you thought it would.

CHAPTER 2

It's Time to Go

There are two moments during a move that aren't mentioned in all the studies and research I looked at: the moment you make your decision to move and the moment you say goodbye.

For one reason or another, you were presented with an opportunity to move to a new and totally unfamiliar place. Maybe you've decided to explore and try to find yourself by making the move solo. Or you're taking the leap and moving for love and adventure. An academic or career opportunity could be calling your name. No matter the reason, you've weighed the options. You've considered what parts of your life will shift, and why moving is the best decision for you to make. You're excited and nervous for the future and all the things you'll create. We call that nervcited.

Even if the move was prompted because of someone else, I hope you acknowledge your decision to follow through. It's a meaningful decision, and a decision some people pass up. I know you know we are privileged to do this moving thing, but for a moment, it's important to acknowledge all the things that brought you to this step. It's a risk you took that will forever alter your life story. I'm proud of you for giving yourself a chance.

The Decision to Move

To understand how I came to my own decision to move, it's time to give you more details on how my husband and I came to be. We met in 2008 in Buffalo in the same business program. I was eighteen, he was twenty. From the day we met, there was something between us. A pull straight from the middle of my chest. A calm feeling that confused me. At the time, I wondered, Why does he like me so much? This can't be right. It wasn't the *Oh my gosh I need him to like me!* obsession I was familiar with in my teens and early twenties that I equated with finding "the One." Because I didn't realize that the calmness and ease were actually a good sign, I was noncommittal after attempting to date for a short time. Just like I ran away from myself in my hometown, I ran away from really facing myself with him. After we graduated, we stayed in touch when we could, seeing each other if our paths crossed in various cities we traveled to over the years. Our awkwardness and that pull from my chest was always there. Somehow, we created enough of a connection that we never lost touch.

While that friendship was developing over the years, I was also busy exploring my relationship habits and choices with my life coaches. Just what was my problem, exactly? I got clear on the kind of partnership I really wanted, the type of man I wanted to be with, and the woman I wanted to be as a potential spouse. I was trying to prepare myself for that one cosmic Hollywood moment I had to believe I would reach. And then one afternoon, sitting in my Toronto apartment in 2018, it hit me like a bolt of lightning. I said to myself, *Rachael, what are you doing? This man you've been making lists about, envisioning, praying for, and feeling is already here.* The friend from university was a match to all those things I wanted. He was my person.

I debated and anxiously deliberated my next move. A month

later, too afraid to make an actual phone call, I sent a long WhatsApp message to this man that changed everything. I said I was sorry for assuming I had a chance at inserting myself back into his life this way, how crazy I sounded, and that I would understand if he said no to my admission of love. I expressed that I was finally ready if he was willing to give me a chance. Now, my husband is a very confident and reasonable man who doesn't let people make a fool of him. I was prepared to be told to leave him alone, but I was also holding on to hope that we still had a bit of magic in our corner despite my flakiness. Luckily for me, he indulged my advance. Four weeks later, I was on a plane to Dubai so we could see if we felt in person what we could through our calls and messages. This trip would mark the first time we'd seen each other in over a year.

In my mind, this was that potential cosmic moment I had done all that preparation for. Another gut check scenario, although this was bigger than a *Should I move here?* gut check like I had on my way to Toronto. This time, it was a *Is this my husband?* gut check. No pressure. I knew in my heart that if we both felt the same way, we'd end up married, and probably pretty quickly, which meant my move would happen quickly too. My anxious excitement built as I tried to relax on my thirteen-hour plane ride. Nervcited again.

As the captain announced we were beginning our descent into the Dubai airport, I had a strange feeling. *That's weird*, I thought, *Why did it just feel like I was going home? I've never been here before.* A calm, cool feeling of *Yes, this is familiar.* The call of the next right step. I deplaned ready to face whatever my future was about to give me. That night, after our initial awkward hellos and trying to act as if we didn't know that everything was riding on my visit, I knew that I was with him, exactly where I was meant to be. Sitting in the backyard of the home I would move to six months later, I knew it was right. That peaceful feeling of home I'd been searching for was also a feeling I experienced in his presence. We both knew it. I enjoyed ten days there with him before it was time to go back to Toronto, agreeing only that I wouldn't renew my lease when it was up in August a few months later, and we would do long-distance until we had a solid plan. Another lease left broken for a new adventure.

I'm Moving When?!

When my now-husband visited me in Canada that June as a part of our long-distance plan, he proposed. That was part of the plan, and it was a beautiful moment. It also was shortly after that moment we realized we didn't really feel like planning another "getaway" for one or both of us as an excuse to meet. It finally seemed like the next logical step was to get married and start our new life in Dubai.

The reality hit me. I wanted to start that life with him, and I wanted to spend more time with family and friends, too. The reuniting of our relationship had seemingly just happened to them, and all of a sudden I was telling everyone I was getting married and moving across the globe. I felt pulled in two directions. After some tears, I had to ask my new fiancé for what I needed. I needed to stay back a little longer, even if it wasn't what we originally agreed to. I explained that it felt like the best way for me to feel complete with my chapter in North America, and we decided he'd come back again in September to move me over. That was almost three months, our longest time physically apart as a couple. But it was just the right amount of time for me to emotionally prepare.

You may have had way more notice—or less—but however long it was, that decision to buy the plane ticket made the move more real to me than before. There are so many deliberations you have in your head before you make that purchase. Thoughts like *What will people think of this? Everyone's going to worry. Am I hurting people? Do I really want to be so far away from my family? What if something happens to them? What about my cat? How am I going to move everything? How different are the laws where I'm going? The food? Can I get by in my language? Do I need a whole new wardrobe? Are their worries about me being safe true, should I be worried?* The list goes on and on.

Google Isn't Always Your Friend

The answers to these questions running through your mind before you make your final choice are not always well informed by news outlets and the latest headlines. You'll find people's opinions about every city on the planet, including the very city you're leaving. I say avoid them if you can. To discover more about what day-to-day life is in the place you're going, whether you've already decided or not, try to find a way to gather information on a firsthand basis. Blogs, online groups, and even messaging people on social media will give you more current and real feedback about what life is like in the place you're considering. Ask multiple people if you can, because everyone has a different experience—and you might just catch someone on a day they get a parking ticket and lean a little negative on the story.

The bottom line in what you're considering is to check in with yourself when you have these fear-based questions. Ask yourself and your heart, does this feel like truly the best decision for my life—and if you're a parent, for my family—right now? If you're here reading, I have a feeling you've already said yes. Consider the problems you might encounter in your new city, and learn what other people who move there do to mitigate them.

Sharing With People Who Care About You

Once you've made your decision, it's time to tell other people about it. Not just in a post on the internet so followers you don't really know are excited for you and reinforce your decision, but the people who might make you the most anxious to tell—those closest to you. You're excited, but also may be a little afraid of hurting them, making them upset. Their questions or disagreement with your choice may be something you have to prepare for. Many, if not all, will be supportive. They'll be sad and show it or they will try to hold it all in, depending on who they are. They are scared for you, and also for themselves, having to adjust to you not being there in the way they're used to.

In a move like this, some of the emotions are yours to work with and respond to, and some of them are not yours to take on. Try to remember that. Some friends and family may also think you're crazy, because it's not a decision they would ever make for themselves. They'll ask questions and want to understand all the details. What's the timeline? What's the place like? What will you do? How will you be treated there? Are you sure that it's safe? (No but really, are you sure?)

For my family and friends, it was a double whammy of surprise and questions about my choices. Very few of them knew my husband and that we'd known each other for ten years, so they were more curious and not so subtly holding back their concerns about how everything was "happening so fast." Marriage and moving? Don't you maybe want to think about that a little longer? Why are you rushing?

This is where trusting yourself and your decisions comes in extra handy, but I'll admit that my anxiety spiked here, and I wondered if anyone had a point. I knew at the core their concerns were coming from love—what would I do if there was an emergency? What if my "new" relationship failed and I was stuck on my own? But when I got down to it and asked myself those questions, I knew I trusted how I felt and that no matter what happened long-term, it would work out. I wasn't going to choose not to experience all the love and joy that was possible because of the possibility of pain. If we know something in our hearts, we have to put that above all else.

And then there were cultural questions about the location itself—things like could I drive (yes) and did I have to cover my hair? (no) It turns out, moving abroad created an opportunity for me to help other people understand and be curious about educating themselves about other places in the world. I admit I was a bit surprised at how many people actually asked me these two questions over and over again, and at times I wanted to pull up a map or Google and explain things that seemed obvious to me.

Get to know the rules and customs of the place you are going and learn through sharing them with the people around you. Just like that, you are impacting history because you are influencing the thought processes of the people who care about you. You are making a huge difference through your one "little" decision.

Wherever we go, we are blessed with the chance to help share more about new places and people through our stories.

—

How Do We Say Goodbye?

As you're preparing to say goodbyc to these people who care about you, it's important to know yourself and the best ways for you to express yourself. I love to write, and I wrote cards after approaching the weeks leading up to my departure with the questions *Have I said everything I wanted to say? Does our communication and this letter feel as complete as it can be?* Of course, it's always a good practice to share important sentiments to family and friends out loud, too, though I still find this a bit of a challenge depending on who it is. I asked some family members and friends how they felt about the ways they'd like to stay in touch and how often, at least as I was first settling in. It was a relief for both of us each time that conversation happened, and we appreciated communication expectations being directly addressed in order to eliminate pesky assumptions. The letters and cards are great keepsakes for your family and friends. Communicate in the way that feels best for you. Even if its uncomfortable, will set you up for easier transition later on.

Your Work and Plan for Arrival

At the time of my move, I was self-employed, still doing my work for online businesses and coaches. Around July I finished up the last contract I was working on and had two months off to prepare myself for the move. My husband and I agreed I'd take one to three months off from trying to find any new clients in Dubai so I could get myself acclimated there as well. This was a great thing—my first time not working in sixteen years, a dream!—but also possibly contributed to why the transition hit me so hard. If you're moving and planning to take time off work or to take the chance to start your own brand or business, that leaves a lot of time for self-reflection in your new home. In my case, that led to a serious identity crisis—but more on that later.

If you're moving for your career or to a job that's waiting for you, ask your employer about their relocation resources before you move. They may offer counseling, legal advice, and connections to networking or even direct introductions to others like you who have relocated recently. See if their human resources department is willing to offer recommendations. This is true even if your spouse is moving for their own job—relocation assistance will extend to you. Don't delay on making use of this resource or even doing your own research to connect with someone before you go. It's okay to ask for help.

Packing Up Life

Let's not forget the emotions that come with packing up your life. Packing can be both liberating and sad. I was cleaning out a studio apartment in Toronto of mostly IKEA furniture, so organizing, selling, and cleaning the place was a lot to manage but also quite simple. Small items reminded me of the journey I'd gone through in my short two years there—the moments in the beginning when I didn't know anyone and had gone to my first couple networking events. There were the retreats I went on and yoga sessions I had at the studio I could walk to in my beautiful tree-lined neighborhood. The half-burnt candles and Palo Santo sticks I used during meditations where I really felt myself and my heart. Those moments I was unsure if I would find love the way I wanted to find it. Journals full of words of excitement, frustration, and anxiety that by the end of the free writing always turned into love and remembrance that we (the Universe and I) would figure it out together. Clothes that made me feel like myself and clothes that were no longer part of the woman I wanted to be. Books half read and some with words written all over the margins.

I packed up all of the life that led me exactly to this point in my journey. That life fit into two suitcases, many garbage bags, and totes. Some of my things went to a young girl who was just starting university and moving into her dorm. Others went to a family with a small daughter who needed to organize her toys. And as if by magic, the last person to come and pick up the furniture they were buying from me was a woman who'd immigrated to Canada from Dubai. We talked and talked and by the end had hugged goodbye, as if our spirits were trading experiences and more fully aligning with the places we were meant to be now.

Be sure to ask for help in this stage: with packing, or for company while you meet anyone who's buying furniture off you, or for someone to pick up food for you while you try to sort out all your emotions. It's easy to feel overwhelmed here. That's okay.

We Probably Won't Get All This Right

Planning the logistics of your move while also planning your goodbyes can feel a bit like a blur with so many emotions and steps to consider. Do your best to stay present. To really be with the person in front of you as you're visiting and saying goodbye. Let people know you see them, you appreciate them, and you love them. Even if you feel happy to get away.

It's easy to talk about the practice of staying present. But here are a few things that I've found that actually help:

- **Wiggling my toes.**
  Being conscious of wiggling your toes when your mind seems to have drifted off really helps bring you back to the moment!

- **Thinking of three things I'm thankful for.**
  Why did we make gratitude practice so complicated? I wasn't doing it because I didn't have time to journal! But that's an excuse. Saying them in your head as you lie in bed at night, in the morning, or as you're drifting into worry really helps.

- **Stating obvious things about my surroundings.**
  My shirt is purple. The sun is out. It's raining. I'm here in my dad's house with him and my husband. Making these statements in my head cuts the future-tripping and reminds me of what's happening NOW.

For me, the tears finally came at a going away party, saying goodbye to my best friend. Up until those goodbyes I was concentrating on practical matters, handling everything we needed to do and worrying more about how my family felt and what they were going through. Seeing my best friend stand up to leave was the hardest moment of my day.

There's a good chance the time you spend with people before you leave won't feel like it's enough. There will be somebody you wished you got to see again or talk to longer. It'll be the "last time we see you until . . ." whenever a visit may be. Those statements are a way for us to reassure ourselves that there will be a reunion at some point.

Throughout my own process, my husband pointed something out to me that I mentioned earlier. Your moving journey impacts you, and you're also impacting the lives of others. Changing their reality. Look at all the ways your one decision has changed the world around you. That's not a bad thing, but it's a reminder for us humans, who can often think of ourselves as insignificant or like our lives haven't been too groundbreaking. They are. It will be difficult to say goodbye to the people you love. We can't take that pain away from anyone, especially ourselves. And if we know in our hearts we need to move, we can't stay either.

Give long hugs. Look people in the eye when you say goodbye. And trust your heart.

If You Learned Only This

- Making your decision to move is a big one. Take a moment to acknowledge yourself for doing it.

- Some blogs, social media groups, and connections, as well as smaller organizations can be reliable ways to learn about the place you're moving to.

- Avoid reading too much news so you get a more balanced perspective.

- You and the people who care about you will go through every emotion there is in the time leading up to your move. Focusing on yours will make it easier to walk with others in theirs.

- Your entire family and friend group will be influenced by the new things you share about the place you live. That's a beautiful responsibility.

- Do your best to ask *Have I said everything I want to say?* before chatting with your friends and family. If there's something, say it or write it.

Write It Out

1. Write out the clear reason for your decision. What benefits do you see of moving? Why have you decided to take this risk? Then say thank you to yourself for taking a chance.

2. Write letters, cards, or messages to the friends and family you might not see for a while. What do you appreciate about their support? What do you love about them? What will you miss and what do you look forward to? What are you feeling frustrated about still? Write versions you will never send, and versions you share.

3. Write a letter to yourself about all the things you have gone through in this place you are now moving away from. You are not the same person you were, and that version of you needs to be acknowledged for getting you to this place.

4. Write letters to the places you have lived—the apartments or homes or the couches you've crashed on, and the cities you have called home. What have they given you or taken from you? How have they loved you and hurt you and changed your life?

5. Remember that it's never too early or late to write these letters. And it's never wrong to write more if you realize you have more to say.

Thoughts to Help You

Say Them as Often as You Need.

- I trust myself and my ability to make the right decisions.

- Everything I'm feeling about this move is okay. Even overwhelm, grief, anxiety or sadness are here to show me I'm simply making a big change. I am normal.

- I am connecting with the people in my life with my heart as open as it can be.

- I am responsible for my decision, and I have nothing to prove.

- If there's anything I forget to do or say, I will figure it out.

It may be that the satisfaction I need depends on my going away, so that when I've gone and come back, I'll find it at home. —Rumi

CHAPTER 3

A New Beginning

And then you arrive. You've landed in this place that perhaps you've only been a tourist in before—or maybe you've never been at all.

For the first few weeks, this part of the journey feels almost like a vacation. There are new cafés and places to discover, bags to unpack, an apartment or home to settle in to, and you can probably take a little bit of time to exist on a flexible schedule. You're friendly to strangers and excited to hear their stories or perhaps find others like you who aren't local. In this stage we're often still connected to the truth of the once-in-a-lifetime opportunity we've stepped into and feel really good about that. Other people can only dream of this kind of experience! In my case, it was rare for anyone in my family to travel out of the state, let alone outside of North America.

Is This a Holiday or Real Life?

Thoughts in your New Beginning are typically things like, *This is so great; there's so much to explore! I can't wait to show everyone everything and share about what I'm doing!* or *I thought moving would be harder, but this isn't so bad; I'm loving it!*

I felt so excited about the journey that was about to unfold; a fresh start—that amazing life I'd planned to step into. I was hopeful for what my husband and I would experience together, the places we'd go, the adventures we'd have. I was excited by the opportunity to redecorate the house I was moving into, to get the chance to make it feel more like home for us.

The first night I arrived, I was so jet-lagged and determined to settle in that my husband and I unpacked all of my stuff then and there. In the days to follow, messages in our family WhatsApp group were filled with photos of our neighborhood, the local Tim Hortons coffee shop we spotted that reminded me of Canada, and all the places we were going out to dinner. We were sharing moments of our every day to stay connected while everything was so brand new.

Acting Fine

There are many things you can do in your own New Beginning to set yourself up for a successful emotional transition. But it could be going so well that you don't realize you should do much at all. For over a month, it didn't occur to me that anything major had just occurred. There was a part of my psyche that didn't quite absorb that I wasn't going back to North America—potentially ever.

I'll be the first to admit that I'm blessed to have moved to a place with almost all the kind of first-world amenities and glitz and glam I could have imagined. If I wanted to, I could never learn Arabic and get by in Dubai just fine. This move wasn't as much of a culture shock as moving somewhere else in the world. But even if you're moving to other sides of the same country, there's still an emotional shift that's happening because your familiar life is gone.

The time when things are going well and we're chugging along as if everything is perfect is actually the time we most need to reinforce the habits that are good for us. Otherwise, a future downswing in life hits a bit harder than it needs to. I was enjoying going out and eating whatever and wherever I wanted. As I eased out of the excitement of the New Beginning stage and moved into the Acting Fine stage, my morning routines of meditation and journaling quickly went out the window. At first because of jet lag and then because it was the first time my husband and I had woken up in the same place together every day. I found myself staying up later than I usually would, getting up later, and then missing a whole morning of my foundational practices. My physical activity routine completely disappeared. Redecorating, managing visa and banking paperwork, and all the other things I had to get in order were the only structure I had. Slowly, I could hear my gut telling me I was getting off track. But I was too caught up with the novelty of everything to listen.

When you first arrive, enjoy the newness and excitement. Take it in and do all the fun things you want to do. Maintain the processes you know support you, if you're able. But if you're not, that's okay too. You'll be challenged to find them again soon, don't you worry.

There are two things in this stage that I would've done earlier to help support my transition process, and they both involve creating tangible representations of putting roots down: one in your own home, and one in the community outside.

Inside Your Home

Your physical home is important, and there will be lots to do. Rooms to fill and decorate with items you may have with you or have to buy all new. In all of my fourteen moves, the one thing I've always been good at and loved doing is making a cozy space. When I lived in New York City, my first apartment in Queens was already lived in by others—I was just renting a room. That room became the safe haven that felt good to me. When I finally moved into my own place in Toronto, I couldn't wait to head to thrift stores and IKEA to find décor and candles. To me, candles, a nice blanket, and a cup of tea make me feel settled and less anxious, no matter where I am.

Why overwhelm yourself thinking you have to finish your entire apartment or home right now? To help yourself settle in, choose one room or even one section of a room to completely finish putting together the way you like it. As soon as you can. It's not just about wanting to buy new pillows and blankets; it's how it feels to see something complete. This new space will hold you and your life. The things we're surrounded by influence our mental state. Treat your home with the respect that you deserve.

For example, I had fun setting up our bathroom quickly with colorful towels, rugs, soap, and toothbrush holders from local shops. Set up a corner in your bedroom with a carpet, some pillows, and photos of your family so you can sit there in the mornings and read or write. Seeing the faces and memories of people you love around you makes a difference. It doesn't matter what room you start on and it doesn't matter what it looks like, just that it makes you feel good when you're in it. Slowly and surely, expand that feeling further into all the corners of your new home. The energy of your home will carry you when you need it most.

Home Away From Home

To begin to feel more settled in your neighborhood, find a café, art gallery, bookstore, or yoga studio that you like. Any place you feel good walking into and that supports you, even in a small way. Avoid picking places like a retail clothing store or a bar/lounge. Keep going back to the place you choose. Keep going until the people who work there start to recognize you and say, "Hello, welcome back!" Have conversations with them and speak to them by name. This will be the first place that feels familiar outside of your home. Little by little, try new places like this to expand the radius of your comfort zone.

I actually learned this trick from my husband. When we first arrived in Dubai, I could never understand why almost every day after work he would go to this same restaurant and café. I'd think to myself, *Can't we go somewhere else? I'm in a new place I want to explore!* But the more he explained, and the more I observed, I began to understand. My husband has moved many places across the world since university, and in each city, he found a place like this to go. On his own, with his entire schedule consisting mostly of work, he decided to create places of familiarity and comfort. So, finally taking a move from his playbook, I tried it myself at my own favorite café. And I got it! I keep going back there, and many of the words in this book were typed seated at the booths where they now know I prefer to sit. Sometimes being a creature of habit has benefits.

Find a place like this early in your Acting Fine phase, and you'll begin to sow the seeds of a physical home and community for when you need to feel them most. Take it in. Take pictures. Document the memories. Share them if you feel like it. It's all part of the journey.

I loved my first few weeks finding my way so much. I couldn't have expected that just a month later, my birthday would be the trigger for everything to come bursting out.

The Moment It Hits You

At first, it was like every other day in Dubai for me. Quiet, sunny, birds chirping outside my window. Because of the time zone, there were very few birthday calls and messages to wake up to. I shook off the "Did everyone forget about me?" thought and got out of bed to prepare for the day my husband planned—an overnight at a beautiful local hotel and spa. And then I saw an email from my aunt with a link to a video. I braced as I clicked to see her with my grandparents. Singing "Happy Birthday" and donning a cowboy hat, my grandfather made his best effort. My grandmother sang at the top of her lungs with excitement as they all exchanged laughs and tears from the fun they were having, wishing me the happiest birthday. In that moment, it suddenly hit me: I was so far away from everyone. I immediately burst into tears. This birthday reminded me of how much love was there for me in North America, and that I couldn't hop in the car for a quick visit.

It was the first time I could no longer deny there was no going back. As I wiped my tears, I heard my mother in law and a family friend downstairs. They arrived with a beautiful cake, gifts, and flowers. I felt like had to pull myself together. To grin and bear it even though I don't like doing that anymore. Everyone wanted me to feel loved and happy, and I was unable to put into words just what I was feeling. My life was perfect, but inside I felt like something was falling apart.

This point in the journey is just that—a split-second as you're going about your day when you finally recognize all that's happened, where you really are, and that your reality has completely changed.

There's not much you can to do prepare for this quick moment. We have to let ourselves be. To cry, to surrender. You may grin and bear it for a while like I did. That's okay. It's the beginning of an important process of growth. We can't protect ourselves from pain, as much as we try to make sure we've got all our bases covered and all our to-do lists made. No matter how hard we try to have "control" and plan and establish healthy boundaries. Life happens. So, we let it be.

On Being Happy

My sadness awareness birthday revelation meant I had to return to baseline ways of taking care of myself. Start over again. The moment it hits you is a humbling moment. But as experience tells me, starting over means looking at what I've really been feeling, taking baths, reevaluating my thoughts, and asking for help. Our minds can be tricksters, and my thoughts were leaning on the heavy side.

Since I didn't seem to be happy, the first thought I decided to look at was what "happy" actually meant to me. I'd never really thought about it. What was I comparing myself to? What rule book or grading system was I using then to decide how I wanted to feel about myself? Was it a truthful, loving grading system? Or was it something else?

What became clear was that I was defining happy through two criteria. First was the way I thought I wanted my life to be: a fulfilling relationship with my husband, always feeling connected to my family and friends, working and writing in a way that felt expansive to me, a picture of perfect health, and setting the foundation for raising a family. And we all lived happily ever after. No pressure, right?

The second way I formed my definition of happiness was through other people who seemed to be living the life I wanted and described in criteria number one. Everyone around me seemed like they were happy. Were they happier than me? People in Dubai seemed to be having thriving businesses, and the women who had kids also looked fabulous, as if they were never stressed.

As I stared at these two criteria in my journal, I said to myself, *Okay, Rachael. This clearly isn't working. First of all, you know everyone has uncomfortable parts of their lives. And realistically you know you'll be wanting new and different things for the rest of your life. If you achieved everything you've ever wanted right now, guess what you'd be the rest of your life? Bored and unhappy! So how can we adjust the way we feel to allow ourselves more room?*

The transition of a move requires giving ourselves grace. This conversation with myself is an example of what offering yourself that grace can look like. Asking yourself the right questions in your journal is a great place to start.

Being kind and loving to yourself involves looking at how you can give yourself the support you need and not expecting to always get it right first time.

—

My New Definition of Happiness

Eventually I came to my own definition of happiness. Here's the adjustment I came up with. It's given me more space to be happy even in small moments every day in my life rather than chasing the destination of a perfect life in my new home.

Being happy means understanding that things aren't always going to feel perfect and wanting to do life anyway. Even though it's scary to have so much be unknown.

Being happy means knowing yourself enough to know what your options are to help yourself out of a stressful or darker time (part of which includes asking other people for help).

Being happy means you've created a support system of people and of things that can carry you while you're feeling all your feelings.

Part of being happy is letting yourself feel really bad. It's giving yourself grace and permission to have a few hours, days, weeks, or longer to sit with what you're feeling.

Being happy can also coexist with mental illness. They are not mutually exclusive, because happiness is not a constant state or feeling. We flow in and out of feelings in a matter of seconds. And honestly? We wouldn't comprehend the sensation of relief, of joy, or of excitement unless there were other emotions to experience in contrast. If we were traditionally "happy" all the time, eventually happiness would get boring. And you are not boring. You're an amazing, multidimensional human being.

All of these definitions of happiness are things we can work towards. You might not know how to let yourself feel everything all the time, but you can learn new ways. We might not have the exact support system we want, but we can find it.

What Happiness Is Not

To summarize, my definition of happiness is knowing things aren't always going to be perfect and wanting to do life anyway. The really awesome thing about your life is that you get to make up your own version of things based on what feels good to you. Literally—you could disagree with everything I've written and said up until this point and that would be absolutely fine, because it's your life, and you get to take back that power. It's been said before and I'll say it again: what will bring you happiness and joy will not look like anyone else's way. Maybe some similarities, but the finer details? Nope, those are yours.

We've spent way too long as a society defaulting to what other people enjoy, what other people prefer, and *I don't know, you choose*-ing our way through things, even in subtle ways. So, your definition of happiness? Take the time to decide for yourself. It'll give you clarity to know what you're judging yourself against. To help you get started creating your definition, I'll share a few things about what I believe does not equal happiness. It might give you some ideas on what you do want it to be like. Or you can forget everything I said and do it your way anyway.

Happiness is not what anyone else says it is. I know, I said it again. But I've seen some great marketing in the world try to tell people that one expert or life coach's solution is the best and only way to success; the "Five-Step Blueprint To Hack": fulfillment, happiness, losing weight, making money, eating cake, etc. Your life. Your relationships. Your happiness.

Happiness is also not a person, place, or thing. This one is tricky for me to remember sometimes. All of those can give you a feeling of happiness, hence the term "it makes me happy." But they are not happiness itself. It is your observation of the person you love or what they do that creates the happiness you feel. Same goes for certain relationships, kids, cats, dogs, corporate job, self-employment, etc. Those things don't make you happy just by having (or not having) them. It's all about what you do with them.

Happiness is not a constant state or feeling. Ever. Therefore, happiness is not a destination. Not the job, the right partner, the baby, or the dollar amount in your account. Those are nice, beautiful, wonderful experiences. You'll reach that destination and be super excited about it. And then your boss will take a sabbatical and you'll get a new one you'll have to adjust to. You'll have your first disagreement as a married couple. Your baby will grow up and leave the house. All that new money in your account will make you anxious about spending it because what if it never comes back? We reach destinations in order to be challenged to reach a new one. To evolve. That's the point of life. But our accomplishments are not the definition of happiness.

Finally, beware any human you see who has their life figured out on social media. Because even though she posts about how she doesn't have it all figured out so you relate to her, sometimes we let ourselves think she's still better than us anyway. That's a big fat brain lie.

What will your definition of happiness be? How will you claim your life back? Decide now.

I also want to be clear about something. If you are feeling really yucky right now, as in you physically are struggling to function, haven't eaten in a long time, are in a depression that hasn't budged, find yourself turning to unhealthy ways to cope, and/ or have a history of mental illness, then this transition may require that you have more support than you think you "should" need. That is totally normal and okay. Reach out to someone who can help, whether that be a local counselor, an expat counselor, a family member or friend you trust, or even by reaching out to your local embassy if you're abroad. Truly happy, independent people are people who know how to ask for help, and you are not alone in this.

If more than one of the following scenarios apply to you, talk to a professional sooner rather than later.

Some of these were thoughts I had consistently for over a week:

- I don't usually cry this much.

- It's been difficult to concentrate or make plans for the future.

- I've been constantly worried something bad is going to happen to me or my family here.

- I don't think life is worth living sometimes.

- All I want to do is sleep, drink, binge on Netflix, play video games, or scroll online.

- I haven't had a proper meal in days.

If You Learned Only This

- Enjoy the fun of first settling in. This is the brand-new adventure you prepared yourself for and you've still made the right decision.

- Pick a pocket of your new home to completely finish setting up or decorating in a way that makes you feel good.

- Go to the same café over and over until you know the workers by name and they know your order. This feels so good.

- Creating your own definition of happiness is an important first step to releasing any pressure you might find yourself packing on to what you've accomplished.

- Happiness is not a constant state, person, place, or thing, or what anyone else tells you it is.

Write It Out

1. When was the moment you really realized you've moved and you're not going back? Describe the scene, what you were thinking, and how you felt. How do you feel now?

2. What has happened recently where you've been hard on yourself? Where can you let yourself try again?

3. Write out how you want to define happiness. What does it mean to you? What is the most loving way to "judge" yourself?

4. What does not equate to happiness for you? Where can you let yourself off the hook?

Thoughts to Help You

Say Them as Often as You Need.

- I can figure this out, one day at a time!

- It's okay to take a step back and give myself another chance.

- This is really hard right now. I am having a hard time.

- I am willing to let myself have a hard time. I will not try to rush through it.

- My success is not dependent on feeling good all the time. It is dependent on my resilience.

Hiding the
truth from
myself
has never
served me.

But oh,
I do it so well.

CHAPTER 4

Why Is Everyone and Everything Irritating Me?

The thing about that moment everything hits you is that there are signs of it coming. I didn't see them. I know I said I was loving life, because I was. And I was also quietly getting frustrated more quickly or being short with my husband in ways I wasn't used to. Blame started bubbling up. This can look like blaming the city or country for the way they do things, the way their culture is, or frustration with the mess in your not quite unpacked house. When I was feeling really low, I wanted to blame my husband for not asking every day how I was doing. Did he not care I'd made this entire life change for him?! Of course he did, and I knew I made the choice willingly. That turned into blaming myself—for feeling this way, for not doing the things I know I could be doing to take care of myself, for not being able to get out of the funk.

You may not recognize frustration and anger happening until you've skipped over straight into Your Low Point, where depression or doubts about your decision to move creep in. But if you do notice signs of blame, the most important thing to do is to let yourself feel it. To feel the frustration and not try to talk yourself quickly back into all the reasons you're so blessed and lucky to be in your new city. It's possible to feel both completely pissed off and blessed at the same time. Feeling ungrateful doesn't make you a bad person, no matter how many blogs say it's important to practice gratitude. Suppressing your irritations does not make the physical response in your body go away.

Shifting into an Unfamiliar Reality

Shortly after my birthday realization and cry about never going back to North America, I stumbled across an acquaintance's post on Facebook. He was sharing how he noticed he hadn't really been motivated to do much of anything lately. He was feeling tired, eating poorly, and feeling agitated more than usual. He was reaching out for some suggestions. I was curious, and there it was in the comments, staring out at me: "It sounds like maybe you're depressed."

Could I be depressed? I related to what he was describing. From the outside, there were signs—sleeping a lot during the day, not eating well, generally no motivation to do anything, irritability, and crying randomly . . . Why hadn't I noticed earlier? But no, maybe that wasn't it. It couldn't be that bad. I don't get depressed anymore, I've done so much work to prevent it!

Or so I thought. I didn't snap out of it. In fact, one afternoon a couple weeks later, I was visiting my husband's office to take care of some settling-in paperwork with a local bank. As I realized it was time to leave his office and say goodbye, I burst into tears. I didn't know why I was crying, but the tears were poised and ready to come out before I even had time to notice. "I'm depressed," I said to my husband as he looked at me with concern. "There's no other explanation for why I'm feeling this way and I can't seem to get out of it. I feel helpless. I need to do something." The confidence and connection I had with myself when I left Canada seemed to have gotten lost with the luggage on our way over.

I thought I was exempt from ever going back to an overanxious state because I had done so much personal development work in order to never have to feel that way again. I wanted my transition to be seamless. It turns out the pressure I put on myself to have the "most successful move ever" created the very frustration and sadness I was trying to prevent.

Oddly enough, the realization I couldn't just deep-breathe my way out of this feeling was relieving. At least now I had a clue why I'd been feeling so unlike myself. I thought something was wrong with me, that I was just stupid and lazy, unlike everyone else I was comparing my life to. But now I had something to work with. This move was different than the moves that came before it. It required me to muster everything I hadn't realized I'd learned from all the other "smaller" moves, call myself back to my center, reach out to friends and family and learn how to have intimate connections from afar, build a community of my own, and ultimately open up more opportunities in my life than I thought were possible.

I felt lost and anxious as I found myself reacting to myself, my husband, our puppy, and people in general in ways that didn't express gratitude for the life I'd stepped into. And witnessing my behavior made me feel even worse.

Maybe This Was a Terrible Mistake

Here, in this stage, there are often thoughts like:

What am I supposed to do with myself?
I hate everything. This is not what it was supposed to be.
Did everyone just forget about me?
Did I make a mistake?
I need to go back home; I can't do this.
Depression and sadness around moving kicks in when we are

resisting the truth. That everything is different now. Just like the grieving process, we are shedding our old selves, our old lives, and all the old ways that people used to relate to us. We miss our families. We miss the way our friends were in our lives. There is in fact a death occurring to allow for new life. The more we resist this happening, the stronger the discomfort. You must lean into your new identity that's forming. I was no longer the daughter and granddaughter who spent focused, present time in person with my family once a week. I wasn't a single woman walking around impatiently, wondering whether and when my real love would come. I wasn't who I had been for so many years.

Almost overnight I became a woman responsible for our home. I was responsible for maintaining my own happiness while being newly married. And I felt I was failing, asking more of my husband than I should have been. I had to come to terms with the fact that having so many options in life was actually terrifying, and that I was worthy of thriving in this new lifestyle. What would strangers think of me? What would my family think of me and would we be able to relate? I became a daughter- and sister-in-law, navigating multiple relationships within a brand-new international and intercultural family.

You must acknowledge and grieve your experience. The old me was a beautiful part of my story, and I needed to let go of her insecurities and fears. But she didn't want to let go. The North American me wasn't sure we would really be safe. We knew how to respond in our old environment, with the people who were familiar. We had no idea how to respond in the Middle East and if we would be successful at it. We had no idea if we really truly did want to be so far from our family for possibly forever.

Looking at the Icky Stuff

My unease and discomfort had spread out into all aspects of

my life (not just to things related with having moved country), and my brain was listing reason after reason for why I couldn't seem to find my happy. With my new definition of happiness, I logically knew I was supposed to be okay being not okay. But even that irritated me in this stage! What were all the things that were getting in the way of my happiness?

For starters, my husband's job and his relaxation time started upsetting me daily. When we were doing long-distance, our visits meant we were spending as much time together as possible. Now I had way too much time alone on my hands, and when he wanted to come home from work and relax, I found myself waiting for all his attention. All I could think of was, *How dare he not spend every spare second with me after all I've done to move here?* Of course, he would offer his time, but I was putting pressure on that attention to fulfill me, and that wasn't happening. Because no person can do that for us.

Then it was the legal process of doing all my paperwork to open a bank account, get my ID card, and get a license. After that, it was all the "perfect" stay-at-home-mom expats I found on Instagram who homeschooled who made me feel miserable. They seemed so happy! Their whole lives were their families, or their missionary work, or whatever they were doing, plus they found the time to share it all on social media when I couldn't even get out one post a day. How was I ever going to become who I wanted to be in the world if I couldn't get it together to post on social media?!

I blamed my friends not reaching out to check in on me enough—days would go by. Didn't they know how hard this was for me? Why was I the one doing all of the reaching out? After blaming everyone else, my brain turned on me. It was my fault. Why couldn't I just get my life together and be happy like everyone else seemed to? Why didn't I have the motivation to do all the things I know I want to do? Of course I was going to screw this up too, like many things in my life. Exaggerate much? My meany-blame-voice will do that to me, in a not-so-sarcastic way. It actually feels like I'm never going to come out of it.

And then I asked myself something. If my idea of happiness is to know that I can always find my equilibrium eventually, if I know I have and I always will, somehow, then where were all these ideas of blame coming from? All of these thoughts were created because I assumed things like my husband would come home every day and spend a lot (okay, all) of his time with me, that assimilating would feel easy because Dubai is a city with a lot of English speakers and yoga studios, that I would jump right into my work and feel more creative than ever before with all this time on my hands. . . .

And yes, all these reasons I was blaming can in some way be legitimate, irritating, and frustrating to anyone. All our feelings of lacking usually are. But in the thick of it, these thoughts are like a nasty, evil voice or a weight on my chest. I felt like I was failing because I wasn't in a state of bliss all the time in this new place of privilege of living in our beautiful home and country, with an amazing husband, a happy puppy, and more time than I'd ever had in the world to work on my writing. Instead, I was blaming everyone and everything for my "failures."

That Meany-Blame-Voice Is a Part of You

For a long time I was mad at my inner voice. I wanted to just kill her off, never to appear again and always think positively of myself and all people. But like it or not, she's a part of me. Even when she's not actively freaking out, she is a part of me. Forever. In order to come home to yourself, we must find a way to love all the pieces, even the mean ones. Even the ones that seem to throw temper tantrums in your adult mind. And we have to be able to recognize what they're really trying to say.

What was my mean voice telling me? I was afraid of all the un-known territory. Wouldn't it be easier to go back to our single life, bouncing from client to client and unfulfilling scenarios, in un-affordable apartments in Toronto, where we had pockets of hap-piness and joy? Where we know how to handle never quite being where we want to be? After all, almost but not quite accomplish-ing our goals was where this voice and I had grown comfortable with each other.

But handling all the things we've ever wanted? Well, that requires a whole new version of us. A version where meany-blame-voice would have less to worry about and even have time to get her long, black nails manicured after a leech massage, or whatever self-care she's into. She didn't want to let go. It's hard to allow the possibility of happiness if we've gotten used to dis-appointment. So meany-blame-voice blamed my depression on everyone else. She was afraid to admit that the grief of letting go of our old life was overwhelming her.

It took work to calm this voice. I had to sit with my journal and talk to her as if she was another person. Asking her about all the ideas she had on how she thought the move would go, how she expected everyone to act (including me), and when she would let us all off the hook.

Because how can the people we care about please us if we aren't even clear what we're asking them to do? Instead of mov-ing through life without reflection, we need to look at where our expectations are running on autopilot. Before they take control of our joy.

Recognizing Our Expectations

Expectations are strong beliefs that something will happen or be the case in the future. A sibling of assumptions, they can feel both negative and positive, like expecting your favorite flavor of tea will always satisfy you, or that the process to get your bank account in your new country will be a total pain because that's what people on the internet say.

Basically, expectations are what our brains do when we don't actually have facts or know what's going to happen because it hasn't occurred yet. They are our minds trying to keep us safe by telling us exactly what's going to happen or what to worry about, in every moment of every day. It's nice of our brains to want to keep us safe. But when it fills in the blanks of *What's going to happen in _____ scenario?* the information is often skewed— sometimes based on past experience, childhood trauma, someone else's story we've heard through gossip, and even books, movies, and societal beliefs.

Because our brains are constantly taking in that information , all our unspoken expectations grow, mostly without our explicit knowledge. We don't recognize them until they:

1. come true, and we can say, *Of course that happened that way. What did you expect?*, or
2. aren't met and we're sitting around frustrated with ourselves and others.

Expectations are a normal part of our lives, and it's always helpful to expect the best—of every situation, person, and yourself. But if you're feeling particularly grumpy lately, then the practice of checking for faulty expectations can help. For me? Like I said, I didn't realize I was in this state of blame due to my expectations for quite a while. There were a few warning signs. I was getting easily agitated, and I wasn't communicating with my husband as easily and lovingly as usual. When I finally noticed that I had even taken to yelling at our new mischievous puppy, I realized that a lot of my unspoken expectations weren't getting met.

Getting Out of the Funk

If you haven't made your big move yet and you're in the preparation stage, great! You can check all the expectations that've been creating themselves while planning and daydreaming about your new life, and see if they're serving you. Keep this section handy for when you are weeks or months into your move.

Here are some signs that expectations or assumptions are cramping your style on the path to feeling at home:

- Thoughts that range from *Why don't I feel like myself?* to *Everything sucks!*

- Irritation at little things, shutting down, and communicating less with the people around you is happening regularly.

- Sense of humor is lacking from your conversations. Everything feels like one big serious quest to feel back to your motivated self.

- You find yourself complaining (even just in your head if not out loud) more than usual.

- You're feeling frustrated after talking to friends or family because thought you'd feel relieved, but you actually feel worse.

- You're wondering why you ever thought you could have it all.

If you're finding yourself with any of these feelings—and I guarantee there are at least three expectations underneath causing them—then we've got to look at them so we can decide:

1. Where the expectation came from. Was it your own expectation in the first place? Did you hear it from someone else's past experiences?
2. If it's something you still want to assume or expect
3. How to choose a new expectation if it's not helping you feel at peace
4. The best way to communicate your expectations if they involve another person

When our expectations go unspoken,
we don't have a chance to decide
if they're fair or communicate them
with the people (or places) we
want to fulfill them.

—

The only way to work with your expectations is to bring them up, look at them, and politely ask them if they have good intentions. It wasn't until I was able to sit down for hours and list the things I expected out of this move and from the people I love that I was able to let myself off the hook and get into action. With new awareness, I could explain how I was feeling to my husband so he could be more empowered to help me. I could finally send a ten-minute long voice note to my friend in Toronto and share why I had been so shut down without realizing it.

Going through the expectations list allowed me to recognize that I needed to search for wellness spaces in Dubai where women I might actually want to be friends with were hanging out, and create a women's community of my own. I could finally get out of my own way. Turns out, sometimes you have to get things wrong first to know how to get them right.

Everything You're Feeling Is the Perfect Place to Start

Being in this state of uncertainty is the best place to be. It's where you can figure out what isn't working and change it. Even if you're thinking I feel fine about my move, everything's really great!, try the following exercise and see what comes up. Let's walk through three common expectations. I'll share how I worked through the questions to reframe them, and then you'll discover how to uncover other expectations that are specific to you.

Here are some #newplacenewlife expectations:

I know it'll be an adjustment, but I'll settle in quickly!

When I moved to Toronto, I knew no one and found community quickly. I felt settled in a matter of weeks. Because I was confident and had done it before somewhere else, I expected myself to be able to do it again. Three months into my Dubai move when my depression was at its peak, this was probably the assumption causing the most discomfort. The assumption that there should be any time frame on me feeling settled was dangerous. I needed a new outlook. Judging myself based on my previous moves, when my life and location were quite different, was unfair to myself.

Meany-blame-voice thought that our lack of assimilation meant I'd always feel lost. But I had to decide that settling would take me as long as it would take, and that would be okay. Every day, if I made a little effort to take care of myself, I'd begin to feel better. I needed to forgive myself for putting pressure on myself. If it was anyone else, I'd support them, no matter how long it took them to feel better, and I would never assume it would happen overnight. To communicate this expectation, I needed to tell my husband and my close family and friends that I had felt so unlike myself because of this faulty expectation, and I was going to do my best to just take it easy.

If you notice yourself carrying the expectation you'll settle in quickly: yes, my love, you will settle in. Absolutely. But dig deeper and see if you have thoughts around how long you've given yourself to feel "settled." I remember getting a message from someone in Dubai who has lived in the city for fifteen years who told me to give it at least twelve to eighteen months until I felt like myself again. At the time I laughed and said, "Yeah, right! I'll do it in three!"

Are you putting pressure on yourself to feel at home quickly in your new place? What if it could take you exactly however long it was supposed to, and you could still be happy during the process? Would you lighten up on yourself a bit?

My communication with my friends and family will stay the same.

I expected that I'd constantly be reaching out to my family and friends, and that they'd miss me and fill me in on their days all the time. In Toronto, I spoke to certain friends almost daily, and saw my family often. I assumed none of that would change, except the seeing part! After some time into the move, when everyone realized I was physically safe, doing okay, and I had sent all the photos and videos I could, communication with almost everyone went from multiple times a day to much less. Some of this had to do with the fact that at times I wasn't feeling up to chatting, and my expectations of constant contact weren't realistic. I needed a new baseline.

With this expectation being unmet, I became afraid people were forgetting about me. I decided to assume instead that we were all doing the best we could, and that we loved each other. If there were really any friendships that were going to end or change, I knew that would only be after I'd made an effort to re-connect. To communicate more efficiently, I told my family that I'd like to talk at least once a week, and I made sure to reach out and plan. I also decided to just reach out to my friends and tell them I missed them!

If you notice yourself carrying the expectation that communi-cation will stay the same, I cover lots of this in Chapter 9, which is on community. But I'll say this: Your friends and family love and support you. Recognize that if you need something or want sup-port, it's up to you to let them know. Take the initiative and share that you're feeling disconnected and want to chat. Life happens, and when distance is involved, it's important to remember that you can still be friends with people you don't talk to, even for months.

We'll go through this whole experience as a couple.

My husband and I are a great team. I assumed we'd go through all the emotions of transition together, but I'd forgotten that he al-ready lived in Dubai for over three years. He was more comforta-ble moving around his everyday life and routine and didn't need support like I did. So we weren't actually adjusting together. I had unspoken expectations of how our days would look, like that he'd get home from work and want to spend every waking moment with me. These unmet expectations made me afraid there was something wrong with our marriage. Clearly this needed some tweaking. To help myself, I decided I was going to assume that my husband and I would go through this together more fully when I let him in on what I was feeling. We also agreed that we would answer each other's phone calls, or at least message when we aren't able, no matter what. This really helped. Finally, I had to decide to take charge of my own schedule. I would no longer work my plans around everything he had to do.

I had to let my husband in on these running assumptions about what our days would look like and recognize that if I had been short with him in some way, it was probably because of these faulty expectations.

If you moved with a partner or spouse, or in fact moved for a partner or spouse, they are hopefully your biggest support system. However, you are two different people and your experiences will not be completely the same. They may feel settled in much faster than you do, or not realize what your feelings about the move are, which can bring up a lot of frustration. Watch for moments where resentment could build and thoughts of *I moved all this way* for you rise to the surface. My husband and I try to figure out a way to communicate what we need and build in time where we're getting out of the house or doing something for ourselves. See if you need that too.

Not going with a significant other? Check in and see what you're assuming dating will be like in your new place, if you're wanting that, or how you're planning to spend your time. If you have a partner who will be long-distance due to the move, see what you're expecting about how often you'll see each other or talk to each other if you haven't planned that yet.

Write It Out

When we make a big move to a new place, we have a lot of unspoken expectations about how things will go. Hopefully, through some of this chapter and my examples, you've already had ideas pop up about what you've been thinking as you've been planning your move or are settling in your new home.

It's your turn to get 'em all out in the open. I suggest returning to this exercise as often as you need to, throughout anytime in your move (or really, your life!). This section of this particular chapter is shaped differently because I think it's one of the most important parts of this book. The exercises will take some time, but take it. You don't have to go through them all right now, or all at once, but commit to visiting at least one section per day.

Simply noticing how you respond will likely make you feel more positive because you'll see that you can be a bit easier on yourself!

Exercise 1:
Brain Dump. Paint the picture you had in your mind.

When planning your move and daydreaming about what life would be like, what were you imagining? What would you do every day? How would you feel? Write out the story.

Exercise 2:
The icky stuff

What are all the scenarios, local laws, barriers, people, etc., you feel frustrated about? Don't worry about being nice. List as many as you have for as long as it takes. Who and what are you mad at, do you hate, do you wish were different? What do you wish would change? Nobody will see this but you.

Exercise 3:
Run expectations through the "do I want to keep you?" questions

I suggest listing out all the expectations and assumptions you can think of and then working your way through the following four questions for each one.

1. Where did the expectation come from? (Was it my own to begin with?)
2. Do I still want to carry this expectation of this person/ place? (Is this reality?)
3. Is there a new expectation that feels more fair or peaceful I can replace this with?
4. Is there anyone I need to talk to who may have been impacted by my reaction to unmet expectations?

Below are ideas of expectations you may have gathered around your big move. This is not a list meant to cover anything and everything, but it gets some basics out of the way and helps you get started. Work through these and add any others you can think of.

Sample Expectations

Of the city or country
- How much do you think you already know about the place?
- What do you expect the language barrier to be like, if any?

- How are you expecting customer service will be?
- How are you assuming transportation will work (public transit, driving traffic)?
- Are you expecting to experience any culture shock?

Of yourself

- How long do you expect you'll take to feel at home?
- Are you assuming you'll feel a certain way through the process?
- How do you expect to feel when you're meeting new people?
- How are you expecting to eat in your first few months?
- What do you think your routine will be like every day?

Of family and friends

- How often do you expect family will reach out to you?
- What will your visiting schedules look like, if any?
- Are you expecting to find new friends in specific places?
- Are you assuming there are or aren't people you'd get along with in your neighborhood?

Of your work

- Do you have any assumptions about your boss?
- Are there any expectations about how long you'll take to get up to speed?
- Are you expecting to jump back into your workload right away?
- Are there any assumptions around how networking and gaining clients will go?
- What assumptions are you making about the job market?
- Are there any assumptions about how you'll feel every day?

Of your significant other (if applicable)

- Are you expecting your partner to check in regularly with you about how you're feeling with the move? How often and for how long?
- What types of activities or events are you assuming they'll come with you on, or even plan themselves?
- What are you expecting your relationship to feel like once you've settled in?

Of your lifestyle or dating life

- Are you expecting dating is going to be hard?
- Are you expecting "all single people" to be a certain way where you're moving?
- What assumptions do you have about where you'll have to go to meet people?

Bonus assumptions to think about

- Of the climate
- Of healthcare and the healthcare system
- Of food, grocery, and dining options
- Of government offices and employees

Are there any other expectations you're holding about you, your family and friends, or your new city you can think of?

This is a very important part of your foundation—if not the most important part: pay special attention to the assumptions you've made about yourself. This is where you are likely to have the faultiest beliefs, even if your meany-blame-voice has been blaming everyone and everything else for the way you're feeling.

Your Expectations Will Fail You

With all your expectations on paper, ask yourself: *Would I place the same level of expectations on my best friend? Why?* Because all these assumptions will fail you at some point. You will fail you. The city and your family will fail you. There's a lot of observing and adjusting that takes place when you make such big transitions like this.

But you knew that. That's why you took this opportunity. You know that the adjustment period is worth the growth, knowledge, and experiences you will have on this journey. You're finding your rhythm. You're discovering who you are again. Allow yourself the same grace.

You've got this.

If You Learned Only This

- Blame, resentment, and confusion are normal in this process. You're going through a huge transition. You are normal and not alone.

- A huge portion of our anxiety when we move is created through expectations we didn't know we had. Asking yourself what they are will help release the pressure and allow you to get more present with yourself and people who can support you.

- Remember to ask yourself:
  1. What am I expecting?
  2. Is it helping me?
  3. Is there something new I can choose?
  4. Do I need to communicate this with anyone?

Thoughts to Help You

Say Them as Often as You Need.

- I'm doing so well. This would be an adjustment for anybody.

- I'm so glad I get to communicate when I'd like something to be done differently and give everyone an opportunity to work together in a way that feels best.

- My way doesn't have to be the only way. I am open to being shown different options.

- I am actually doing and accomplishing way more than I give myself credit for.

CHAPTER 5

What's Your One Thing?

Now that you've been able to see all the expectations and self-imposed requirements you've placed on yourself and others, you're ready to move on from Your Low Point stage. We're going to refocus on what matters to prepare for the next stages of Identity Formation and Thriving. And to refocus, we have to look at how we might feel if living in this new place comes to an end one day. When we're faced with the idea of an ending, we're more able to access what it is we might miss, regret, or wish we did differently.

And since all good answers start with good questions, I'll ask you this: If there was one thing you got out of the experience of living in this new place and that was enough, what would it be? Or, said another way, if you left your new home next week, what would you regret not spending more time doing while you were there?

This could be a short and simple answer, but it's important. And I know you want to accomplish a whole boatload of things while you're there. Why pick just one, right? But settle into your-self for a moment. Breathe and picture your wise, calm, older, and all-knowing self. What would be enough? What do you think may be the main reason you've really moved to this new place? Is there something you're being asked to create, do, or grow through?

Maybe you'd be really satisfied if you showed yourself how

you can adapt to new situations—something that many people from your hometown likely never do. Maybe it'd be enough for you to learn how to get more comfortable interacting with people who speak a different language, or learning a new language itself? Perhaps your satisfaction would come from discovering how the government works in a new place or learning how your business can work in other markets.

Your One Thing can be people-focused, like sharing an experience with your partner and exploring the ever-changing dynamics of your relationship, or making one really good friend you would've never met anywhere else.

My One Thing is to experience connection—to myself, to my husband, to my family, and to the people I meet along the way. If I can regroup, take care of myself after chaotic days, and reach out to my family and friends and feel like we all know we love each other—no matter where we are in the world—then that's enough for me. I want to experience the idea that love and connection are infinite, regardless of physical location.

If I stay in line with this idea, then I am satisfied. All the business stuff, this book, the women's gatherings, the language learning, the food-tasting—those are bonus factors that occur when I am staying true to this idea.

But when I first got to Dubai, I stepped off the plane with the expectation that everything in my life would come together perfectly because of my fresh start. The minute something didn't go my way, it felt like the end of the world. Returning to my North Star of connection helps me remember what really matters to me.

What's the One Thing for you? Let this One Thing be your guiding light, your reminder of what matters. If you are focused on this one accomplishment or area of growth for yourself, the other things that might be happening around you are simply part of the journey, but they are not the reason you're creating this new home.

Your One Thing may change over time, but hang your current version up somewhere in your new home as a reminder. Every few weeks, move it to a new place. After a while, we stop looking at things on the wall or reminders we've scheduled to pop up on our phones. We get used to the encouragement that's right in front of us. So, take the time to remind yourself what your goal is often.

You may be surprised by what you discover is most important to you now. That's okay. A move will shift us when we least expect it, right when we thought we knew everything about who we are. It will open up versions of ourselves we thought we grew past and versions we didn't know we had in us. The resilience and confidence required simply to get through the day means we begin to walk more strongly through the world.

How Do You Define Yourself?

The biggest factor contributing to my depression was not understanding who I was anymore. I remember a few weeks into my move lying in bed and saying to my husband, "What is the point of me? Honestly, who am I and what am I supposed to do?" Being given the opportunity to take time off work and figure this out felt like a dream at first, but when I was knee-deep in spare time, a huge part of me wanted to resort to taking literally any job I could so that I'd have some purpose and something to do.

We attach some labels to ourselves and others are given to us, but how we identify with them is what matters the most.

Which labels make us feel good, and which make us shrill with shame or disgust? Our roles and labels as blogger, mom, yoga student, or account manager—whatever you'd say to someone when they ask you "So what do you do?"—are not the whole story.

It's so important that we take a look at how we feel about certain labels and words. And to look at where those beliefs come from. Are they what we want? Are they serving us? Where can we release the shame and guilt, if there is some, so we can surrender to the reality of who we are? (Even words like *expat, immigrant, nomad,* or *bicoastal human.*) Which labels make us feel proud? And are there any we need to replace?

Who Are You Arriving as, and Who Do You Want to Be?

Even if you're moving to your new city because of a job with the same company, there are many new aspects involved. New people to meet, new employees and new colleagues. But the beauty of meeting new people means you get to decide what parts of you to bring into new relationships. We often decide to embrace changes like these with a little bit of hope that some new part of us will awaken. A more peaceful, happy and expansive part of us.

Have you thought about which new and improved parts of you you've hoped will awaken? They are likely tied to your One Thing you hope to get out of the move itself. It could be that you want to be more open to saying yes to that after-work office hangout. Or that you want to take some of your time to move your body every day in a way that feels good to you. In your old home, maybe you labeled yourself as introverted, and now you want to pick up a bit of an adventurous identity.

Maybe you want to be more of an artist. More of a risk-taker. Maybe you want to be open to finally meeting that life partner and be a spouse or embrace an ability to go with the flow. Some of the labels you had in your old home won't be relevant to who you are anymore. Depending on where you're moving, people might not know what your old job title even means!

What will you hold onto if the labels of your current identity are past their sell by date? What will you say when someone asks you what you do? Can you learn to be comfortable in the space of "figuring it out" like I was? Admit you moved because of your partner, or because you wanted to extend your career to a new place? As you might've noticed, your move is not only a physical move. It's an opportunity to change your way of being and go deeper into your relationship with yourself.

You make the rules. Those job titles, industry names, and family roles are important to claim. But there are new labels out there that can describe you well you haven't thought of.

If You Learned Only This

- You don't have to figure out every detail of your life right now. Choose One Thing you'd love to accomplish while you're in your new home. Let that be your guiding light.

- The outcomes of your decisions don't determine your self-worth. Work to have strong roots and trust yourself, rather than be blown about by other people's opinions.

- How we label ourselves can limit us or empower us. Do you feel resentful when you answer the question *So tell me about yourself?* Use your One Thing to help describe your essence.

Write It Out

1. If you left your new home next week, what would you regret not spending more time doing while you were there?

2. Are there any ways you can start doing more of those things now?

3. Make a list every day, or at the end of every week, of every little thing you accomplished—including getting up or getting dressed in the morning. You're worth it!

Thoughts to Help You

Say Them as Often as You Need.

- I don't have to accomplish everything right away. I have plenty of time.

- I'm actually doing way more than I've been giving myself credit for.

- Returning to my guiding statement helps me remember all this can be easier than I'm making it seem.

- My self-worth is not determined by my accomplishments, but instead how I feel about myself.

CHAPTER 6

Who Am I?

Once you've worked out what your One Thing is, it's time to go deeper into the Identity Formation stage. Times of transition—any transition—are moments where our minds kick into high gear with any possible fears and anxieties about ourselves and our lives. It's in those times we are faced with the questions: Who will we show up as? What will people think of us? What is our purpose for getting up and out of bed every day? Where is our community and belonging?

This is a powerful place to be. When we're right in the middle of this major transition in our lives, we have to become even more diligent in working to reframe all the moments we doubt ourselves. For example, when I first arrived in Dubai, I was considered a newly married housewife since I wasn't working. I gave that label and the idea that I "wasn't doing anything" power in my mind. Power to mean something about me.

It wasn't the literal word *housewife* that was creating a problem for me though; it was the beliefs I had around the perception of what the word meant about me. I created a story about how by not jumping right into work, I was the opposite of a modern woman. I felt the weight of invisible people judging me. I was sitting around in a bigger house than I'd ever lived in, thinking about creating something to do in my "free time" because I had the privilege of not worrying about how I was going to pay rent. I made this mean that I was spoiled and lazy. I scoffed at the idea of being one of "those" women who went to get her nails done at 11 a.m. and rinsed and repeated after doing some shopping. I resented the idea that I could "turn into" a mom who stayed home and had children and devoted all her time to them, all for them to leave the house one day twenty years later and leave me empty-nested and alone. These were the stories I had created around one word because of my own family history, some westernized conditioning, and from spending too much time on social media.

Nothing about being a housewife is wrong. There is immense pride and value in such a role. And it's likely, when my husband and I are able to have children, that for some of that time I will step into this housewife role more traditionally.

I was forced to look at all the ways I was judging other women and creating stress for myself because of one nine-letter word. Was I not doing enough? Was I not good enough? What would people think of me now that I am wading in more privilege? What would I think of me if I couldn't come up with a great business by the next time my friends and family asked me what I'd been up to?

Revisiting my One Thing reminded me that my purpose came from what mattered to me—connection. And if I was accomplishing that, it was all I needed. I now had the freedom to choose other labels.

This chapter is dedicated to reminding you of who are and who you're growing into. I've included a series of descriptions you can consider. Read them to remind yourself how powerful you are, even when you feel like you're not living up to the "role" on your résumé or Instagram profile in 150 characters or less.

As you read through, I encourage you to make up your own

labels. Try them on, see if they fit, and if they don't, readjust or take them off. You'll know they work if you close your eyes and imagine using the label to describe yourself to someone new. Do you feel excited, light, and happy when you say it, like fresh air and sunlight is shining on your face? Or do you feel a little bit of disgust or feel your body contract and want to hide? Keep the sunshine.

You Strive to Give Yourself Grace and Space to Feel Things

Whether you're excited, scared, disappointed, irritated, in awe of your life, or any feelings between, you are okay, I promise you. Give yourself the time to express what's going on. Even if your emotions change in a matter of seconds. All the things you're feeling are normal when you're in flux. Other brave people in the world like you have experienced this during moves. That is not to say you aren't special, but to say that you're not alone. Being in a new place, where you know no one, can feel extremely isolating. Especially if you're not working or if you work from home and cafés where you don't get to connect with anyone.

You are loved, in all your emotional glory. Allow this move to force you to practice being kinder to yourself. To become someone who integrates feeling things as a way of life. You'll actually be much happier this way. So many of us spend time avoiding feeling things, repressing or suppressing because it's inappropriate or immature. The point of life is not for it to be joyful and cozy every second of the day. The point of life is to feel all of it. Even in the darkness, how great is it that we're allowed to experience the fullness of existing?

You Re-center After Seeing Someone's Highlight Reel

Don't despair or compare your experience to other people who seem to have this thing down. Especially the travel bloggers and digital nomads who only share the highlights. You will compare, it's natural, but you have a responsibility to remind yourself of the truth. There will always be parts of other people's lives we'll never see. Many times, travel bloggers or experts come to a point where they realize something they've been doing is no longer serving them. That they'd like to make a new life change (perhaps move back to their hometown, leave their "perfect" relationship, or quit blogging.) If you don't re-center to your own goals, you may be disappointed when the person you were following fails you.

You Care Deeply for Your Family and Friends

Being away from family and friends is one of the hardest parts about moving. Thoughts about *What if something happens to them while I'm away?* occur. You'll wonder if you're staying in touch enough, or what some of them are thinking about how you haven't talked in a while. You want to do right by them, and you also want to take care of yourself. There will always be ways we could have done better. There will always be things that are out of our control, because other people are involved.

And that would be true whether you lived away from them or you lived in the next room. As someone who has lost people for many reasons (death and simply growing apart), I can attest to that. The people in your life who care about you want nothing more than for you to be your fullest version of you. To be happy, to be honest about what you're feeling so they can be a part of that sometimes, and to call and tell them you love them. As the great Oprah has shared after spending most of her career talking to people, everyone deep down wants to be seen and understood.

Caring deeply for your family and friends is an honorable and valuable quality. No one can take that away from you. It is part of your essence, and the people around you can feel it.

If you're feeling guilty about being so far away from the people you care about, use that as a sign to do something. Reach out, tell your family why you miss them. Don't stew in feeling guilty and then sorry for yourself. Use feelings of missing people to figure out a time you can plan to visit or see each other again. To agree to send emails instead of depending on calls if that works better for your time zones. Any feelings of loneliness, guilt, and even grief around missing someone can be used as an indicator that there's tweaking to do.

If I'm feeling particularly frustrated one day, I've noticed it's often occurring during a time where I've left messages or calls unanswered. That could be from being busy working and planning for my writing and events. But still, as that frustration builds, one of the first things that alleviates it is catching up with the people I love. Even if it feels like I have "so many" other things I need to take care of. Rejuvenation that comes from connecting with people always makes my work come easier.

One of my very best friends reached out to me about eight months into my move to Dubai and said, "I've been holding in that I miss you. I get upset about the fact that it's not easy for us to pick up the phone and chat. It wears on me and I refused to admit that to myself or you." I was so grateful in that moment that we have the kind of friendship where she felt safe enough to express that to me. It was an opportunity for me to recognize the ways I wasn't feeding that relationship the way I could be and look at why. Was the time zone the only reason we weren't staying in touch?

The truth was, I had made friends and family feel that they couldn't just call me when they felt like it. Instead, they'd often text me first so I could call them, or we had to schedule it in. This started because of limitations on free internet calling, as well as the time zones. But was that the kind of feeling I wanted to have with my closest friends and family? That we couldn't pick up the phone and at least try to call, even if someone might be busy or sleeping and regardless of the "technicalities"?

No. Even with the time zones. Even in the age where we may tend to be more comfortable with sending messages than phone calls. That's not what I wanted to experience and not how I want people I care about to feel. So changes had to take place.

Now, you may have preferences for how you want your relationships to feel. They don't all have to look the same. But because you're a person who cares deeply for your family and friends, you can make a promise to yourself that when feelings of disconnection come up, you pay attention. If there's anything this has made you think of that you can do, do that. Now.

You Have a Great Desire to Build Things in the World

Whether you want to build a small business, a family, an entire empire, or a simple, happy life with books and tea—these are all great things. You're here and you're still reading because you desire more. More than what your family before you had, whether that's in material form, emotional form, or both. You desire to be kind and to make people feel loved. You desire to be fair and to learn about other people. You desire real, authentic conversations. You desire to feel connection and fulfillment like you've lived your life out in the best way you could.

Your dreams and desires are valued. You don't have to have it all figured out right now, you have to know that you're on to something. Anyone and everyone will tell you things you desire aren't realistic. They will even be nice enough to give you the facts, the statistics, and the data to back up all the reasons why it's not possible. They will tell you that it's not something the people of your family, household income level, background, race, gender, or origins "do."

But you? You find examples of stories of someone, anyone, who's a little bit like you and defied the odds. Who broke the rules, and tried despite what others told them. Because you have this pull in your heart that keeps you going.

I struggled with the idea that I could have a successful relationship, have children, and do work in the world that I loved. I believed that I'd have to sacrifice somewhere, or that I would try for them all and then something would fall apart. I had all these crippling fears: that I would ruin my marriage, or that I would have kids and regret it, or not have kids and regret it. I was spinning in circles wanting to believe that my desires weren't realistic. I had seen enough examples and read enough articles about the struggles that women were going through. But that's the thing. I was reading about the struggles. Are there a ton of struggles around being a wife, mother, and businesswoman? Of course. But where were the stories from women who had gone through it well? The women who successfully raised children into adulthood, enjoyed their marriage, and were also doing work they loved? Why wasn't I reading those? So then I looked for them.

Now, there's a voice in my head telling me that this is the impossible standard of the Western world. Influencing us to believe we can have it all while running ourselves into the ground trying to be good parents, maintaining optimal health and diet, making time for date nights and getaways, being the best boss your employees have ever had, connecting with friends. All while having time for nightly baths and exquisite self-care. Of course we are not going to get it perfect.

But the key here is getting quiet with yourself and identifying whose dreams you are after. Do you think you have to do certain things because other people say so? Or when you close your eyes and think about your dreams, does your heart light up at the possibilities in front of you? If your heart is lighting up, then we can figure out what is realistic later.

At the suggestion of my beautiful life coach and wedding officiant, Amanda, I began to search for other women and other stories I could draw from. This also happened to be around the time Michelle Obama's book *Becoming* came out, which was a great place for me to start. Once I began, more and more examples came to mind. And anytime I'm feeling doubtful of myself, I'll look again!

Whatever you desire in the world, it is valid, otherwise you wouldn't be thinking about it. Your move will bring all those repressed desires to the surface. So admit it to yourself and let yourself feel it. Then go out there and find examples. Take them in and read them daily. The next best step to that is to find real-life examples and become their friends. Don't listen to people who tell you to "relax" or consider other options unless they're successful the way you want to be in the area you're speaking about.

You Expand and Grow Through Many Changes, Trials, and Tribulations

You are seriously a rock star for all the stuff you've been through and what you're getting ready to handle, even before having made this major move. You have gone through puberty (a trying time for us all!), you have experienced heartbreak and feeling left out by your friends, you have experienced times when your body wasn't working the way you hoped it would, you have lost loved ones. You have studied for pointless exams, left jobs or gotten fired, experienced childbirth or lost pregnancies, or all the above. You have been abused or questioned if you wanted to go on with life. You have found God, turned away from faith, and perhaps then found your way back. You have found plenty of reasons to laugh and dance and enjoy yourself despite all those things. And you have done all this before, during, and after moving your entire life to a new location! The part of your story where you have relocated is just part of your story. There are all these other pieces and aspects to hold.

If you have experienced even only one of these things, you are incredible. Honestly. The world wants to hear from you—your story, how you did it, why you're choosing to share now and what you wish people would know.

You may be the example someone else needs to see to believe their own desires and lives are valid.

—

You Forgive Yourself as Often as Possible

You're not going to know how to do everything, get everywhere, or function properly in your new home for quite some time. This is hard for everyone, but especially for people who put a lot of pressure on themselves to get things right. Like me.

When you move to a new place, your inner critic can kick into high gear. This is especially likely if you haven't gotten enough sleep, are feeling particularly exhausted or stressed, have been eating a lot of processed foods, haven't been getting enough movement, or had a rough day exploring your new hometown. I remember the first time I tried to drive to a café date on my own and I was twenty minutes late. It could have been a small thing, but the stress I felt in my body overtook me as if something much worse had happened.

Your brain, hormones and nervous system reactions are not always telling you the truth. You are not your thoughts, those powerful and sometimes pesky things that lead to an increase in both positive and negative emotions. I never really understood the idea that we're not our thoughts until I decided to volunteer at one of Deepak Chopra's seminars and meditation retreats in 2011. Watching your thoughts was a concept I had heard so many times before but I had no idea what the heck it really meant. But somehow, this time in meditation, I noticed the thought *Ugh am I even doing this right?* and I paused and decided to respond with *Hmm, that's an interesting thought to have, Rachael* rather than continue to spiral through the list of why my meditation was incorrect. What? You mean I can interrupt myself and actually feel better?

These interactions with yourself were what I have been referring to as the meany-blame-voice, but have in other writings been labeled our "inner mean girl," "negative thought," "ego," etc.

When you think poorly of yourself, how long does it take you to let yourself off the hook and feel better? Depending on what you're thinking about, some of these recovery times may take longer than others. But as you navigate your new home, it's imperative to cut yourself some slack. You have accomplished way more than many people in your family or in the world ever will. Leading the way in your own way, when you haven't been told step by step what to do or how to handle it, is an amazing feat. Be a person who goes through life, does their absolute best, and forgives themselves for the times they fail.

It's resilience that wins. You are one of the most resilient, beautiful people on the planet. And you are not alone. So keep going.

You Are a Powerful Human

You have more influence than you know. Your life impacts the people around you without you noticing. Have you ever walked into a room and instantly recognized when a family member was a bit edgy? Or been inspired by a person you see in public without speaking to them or even getting near them? That's power. You have the same effect on everyone who comes into your world and space. If you want to do good in the world in even the smallest way, it's actually irresponsible to believe that you're not making an impact. You are making a difference simply by existing! If you knew that the way you decided to walk around while you're shopping at the new market you found in town would impact a child who was watching you from the other side of the aisle, how would you carry yourself?

Of course, there are times throughout this transition when we're feeling particularly down that we don't want to worry about how we're impacting other people. We just want to live and get through the day! So wear a grumpy face if you need to. That's the beauty of your power.

Power is not good or bad. Power is the ability to choose to do something in a particular way. It's an ability, a decision you make to believe you have a choice in how you feel. How you use your power is up to you, and that's the beauty of it. But never let yourself believe that you don't have any.

This Is Just the Beginning

You bring all these qualities to each and every thing you do in your life. You wear these labels without even having to get out of bed in the morning. You bring them to your career, your relationships, your parenting, and your quality of relationship with yourself. You could never work again or you could run a huge company—the qualities remain the same. And they are good qualities.

What labels did you choose for yourself? How do you feel about them now? You are awesomeness personified and all that matters is that you think so. The truth is, the world could care less about your to-do list. But how do you make them feel? How do you feel when you go throughout your days? Are you feeling bad about what you think people think of you? When someone asks you what you do or where you're from, be honest. That could mean today you are a writer working on a blog. That could mean you're a mom, end of sentence. That could mean you're figuring it out and giving yourself a chance to do so.

Because the person who says that to me—who replies, You know, I'm not doing anything right now but taking time to figure out what I want to do. I know I'll get there soon—that person is getting all my respect. Without having to explain anything more.

If You Learned Only This

- Your identity will change continuously throughout your life. The move may amplify the feeling of *Who am I?* more than you're used to. That is okay. A question means the possibility of creating an even better answer than you had before.

- Your identity is less about the "easy" labels, and more about the way you behave. Focus on who you are, not what you do for a living.

- Be a person who asks for help when they need it, who communicates honestly, and who takes ownership of their power, including the power to feel down if you need to.

- You are perfect. And you are loved. You can be both of those and still have things you want to do better. Feeling confused about your identity doesn't make those things go away.

Write It Out

1. Before your move, what labels did you use to identify yourself?

2. Now that you're in your new city, how have you been introducing yourself to people?

3. Which of the examples I shared above do you like, and which ones do you feel resistance toward? Why?

4. Declare at least four new statements that describe who you are inside.

Thoughts to Help You

Say Them as Often as You Need.

- I am a person of value simply because I am here on Earth.

- I am happy to be figuring out all the things I need to know along the way.

- Even if I have a bad day, or a bad year, that does not equal a bad life.

- I can be who I want to be.

- I enjoy witnessing others who practice being fully themselves. They are great models for me to see what I can achieve.

You can buy yourself flowers or journal endlessly, but sometimes the greatest act of self-care is communication and expressing yourself.

CHAPTER 7

Honestly, Asking for Help Will Save You

While I was experiencing my depression, and working through my expectations and identity crisis, I had a hard time vocalizing exactly what I was feeling. Those feelings are easier to identify now than it was when I was in the thick of it. So when my family or friends would call to catch up, at first I was saying things like, "It's a bit weird, but it's going okay" or "I slept a lot today. But that's all right, didn't have much to do!" And then we'd move on to the next topic. But as my stress increased, there was a buildup of tension in my chest and a feeling of dread anytime someone called. *Please don't make me talk about how things are going!* I was avoiding sharing at all costs.

After getting off another call feeling like I was trying to rush through it so I wouldn't be found out, I recognized what was going on and had to admit to myself and my family that I was struggling. I remember when I finally started telling everyone. "You know, it's actually been hard for the last week or so and I had a few bad days. I'm not quite sure what to do with myself, and now that my husband is back to his regular routine, I keep getting jealous and resentful that he had so much to do!" Of course,

I immediately felt relieved. The secret struggle was off my chest. Everyone understood, and actually were waiting for me to tell them what was going on because they could feel something was off. Finally, we were all on the same page.

Being Honest with Yourself and Others

It sounds like a grade school lesson, but when you want to feel at home with yourself, being honest with yourself and others is really the number one way. When we're feeling emotions like grief, sadness, fear, anxiety, and even joy, sometimes we want to lie to ourselves about it. To pretend everything's okay or neutral so we don't upset anyone and can focus on our to-do list. But this pretending creates stress in our bodies on top of the stress we're already feeling. It creates tension and tightness that can manifest as physical pain. A dull ache I always had in my neck and shoulders became excruciating during this time for me, and spread to my jaw. These muscles all work together and because of everything I was holding in, the emotional stress manifested physically to a point that no home remedy helped. Pain in this area is always my tell that I'm way past the point of slowing down. It means I've been running on "go" for too long and need to get something out of my system. Being honest is the fastest way to create more healing both mentally and physically. You don't have to be doing great all the time and nobody expects you to but yourself.

This means being honest about:

- How you feel about the move. Admitting all the feelings to yourself.

- How you feel about the move with your family and friends.

- How you feel about the move with the locals and new friends you meet.

- What you don't know about your new city. It's okay to feel like a tourist.

- What you really want for your life while you're there.

- What you're avoiding doing, saying, or feeling.

- What you need to help settle in better.

- What you believe in, even if your new country operates a little differently.

- Who you are and what you're going through if you share online.

- How happy you actually are. Celebrating the joy and allowing it when it appears.

Pay attention to your reactions to others. What you say and don't say will often give you an internal reading around what you're really feeling during the transition. The best place to watch yourself is after you're asked questions like *What do you do? Where are you from?* and *How are you settling in?*

Who you are will fundamentally change after you move to a new city, no matter what. It can feel like a complete identity crisis. This is normal, so it's important to stay true to yourself by letting people in on it. You decide to whom you share or how much you share. A simple *You know, it's been hard today, I'm still adjusting* can be all you need to allow someone to support you.

Deepen Your Communication

Whether we've relocated or not, learning to communicate like an adult is one of the biggest game changers for all of our relationships. This means expressing what we're feeling, maintaining boundaries, and giving others a chance to share their own experiences. When you move, avoiding deep conversation and only focusing on surface-level catch-ups can create disconnection that negatively impacts us in the long run.

When you're being honest with yourself and others about how you feel, your relationship has a chance to deepen. It's harder than it sounds. We may think we're being open, but that's not what's actually being felt by the other person. We can blurt out something in frustration or tell a white lie to save someone's feelings. We might isolate ourselves when we're upset, hoping someone will reach out first. We're humans and we're learning and adjusting. But each moment you try to open up gives you an opportunity to look and say, *Oh, I really could have done that better. How can I try again?* There's that grace for you.

In my own life there were, for a period of time, occasions where

I had no idea how to express myself when I was feeling things (which get this, is all the time). When I was upset, hurt, frustrated—whatever it was, I was often defensive, which prevented me from being able to express myself clearly. This still happens. And moving farther away from people we love can make it easier to just want to stay on that surface. When your time together to connect is limited, we may feel like we don't want to ruin it with "feelings." But over and over again, I've seen that the hardest conversations are the ones that create the most connection.

Here are some thoughts or statements that could indicate you're feeling defensive or avoiding your feelings:

- *I'd reach out to them more if they made an effort too.*
- *Nobody is checking in on me and I don't want to talk to them now.*
- *I'm good, no new updates. How are you?*
- *I knew I shouldn't have talked to you about this.*
- *I'm not being defensive.*

Here's an example of what you could say instead:

- *I need to share something with you. I've noticed that when you get home from work, I'm waiting for you to ask me how I'm feeling and adjusting. I feel really frustrated and sad when you don't, because every day is still hard for me. Can you check in with me before we get busy with other things?*
- *When we don't talk for a week or two, I feel so stressed. Can we figure out a solution?*
- *I'm sorry, I'm feeling defensive and I cut you off. Can you explain what you just said again so I better understand?*

It's scary to be honest and to admit we're wrong or struggling. There are so many opportunities for us to be rejected, to feel rejected (we may interpret someone's reaction as rejection if it's not exactly what we wanted), or to feel like we have made a fool of ourselves. People may laugh. They may disagree with us. They might decide not to spend time with us anymore.

But one of the keys to feeling at home in yourself and then in the world is communicating honestly and openly. Of risking that rejection. Because it's the most freeing feeling when you aren't wearing any protective covering on your heart. And the right people find a way to stay.

Asking for Help

After you've recognized what you're feeling, it's also your responsibility to ask for help. The greatest leaders of our past and present didn't do it alone. This may be one of the hardest things in the world to do, but if you're reading this book that means you're already made the first step. You're maybe reading this book because you want to be and feel the best you can in this lifetime. You want to experience all the things you believe happy people experience. Even though you think you're helping yourself on your own by reading this book, you've also allowed me to join you and support you. And I want to stretch you a bit further.

I still find asking for help a real challenge, but I'm embracing this challenge more and more these days. If I want to create what I say I do—in my life, in my family, and in the world as a whole—I'd be crazy to think I can manage it all myself. From now on, why not be the kind of person who asks other people for help? Even if you can't return the favor, pay them or reciprocate in any way. Yes, really. Other people always have the option to say no. Being able to ask for help is one of the bravest aspects of taking care of ourselves.

Being independent means you know how to be supported.

—

I had that backward for a while. As a teenager and into my early twenties, I prided myself on being independent. From the age of fifteen, I held many jobs, not counting the endless babysitting I did before that. For a long time, my family wasn't in a place where I felt I could ask for money, even though they would want to have helped me if they had the chance. I got uncomfortable asking for anything if I hadn't "worked for it." I told myself that I was a more desirable girlfriend and partner if I paid my own bills, studied on my own, and didn't need anyone for anything. I could figure out my emotions and my relationship stuff myself. I blasted the song "Miss Independent" by Ne-Yo from my car with the windows down. I thought I didn't need anyone, and I was proud of it.

But deep down, I felt alone. I didn't know how to communicate like an adult when I felt I was treated unfairly, or when I was experiencing emotions that dragged me down. I got overwhelmed by the stress of working more than one job at a time. All I could do was complain to others. If they offered advice, it wasn't listened to. I thought I was smart enough to figure it out. This overconfidence in myself was actually a mask. My determination to not "need" anyone actually left me feeling desperate inside for attention. I wanted someone to come and fix all the things in my life without me having to mention what they were.

But the fixing that actually needed to occur was with my ability to accept help. Which brings me back to a memory of leaving a Blockbuster (*ahem*, a place that no longer exists where you used to be able to go and rent movies) with my now-husband. On our way out, he asked to carry the DVDs to the car. Instead of letting him I said, "It's okay, I got it." Ohhhh, how many times in my life I've said those words when I didn't want to "have it." It's such a little thing, but in that moment, I was rejecting help from someone who truly wanted to give it. He cared for me and I was depriving him of an opportunity to feel good, and depriving myself of an example to feel looked after. This silly example was indicative of all the bigger ways I wasn't letting people in my life help me ten years ago. And so many of those people wanted to help, or would have been willing, if I only had asked.

I've worked on this for a long time since then. Luckily, I now love the way my husband feels pride when he can take care of me in some way. Marrying and moving shined a brighter light on where I was going at things alone. When I didn't know how to get somewhere, or when I was feeling really down, I finally had to be honest about my sadness and let people just be there for me: to offer suggestions, directions, and drive me places. To pay for things. To tell me how to support myself in getting out of a funk. To tell me they are here for me no matter what.

What I've learned about independence is this. If you want to label yourself as independent, try tweaking the definition. Being independent means you're smart enough to know when you need help and you are confident enough to ask for it. It means you totally could take care of things on your own, but you know you don't have to. Asking for help does not mean you are weak and can't handle things; it means you're strong enough to know you weren't put on the earth to do everything alone.

Moving to a new place will make doing things on your own

near impossible anyway. So might as well use this time to stretch your ability to embrace support. Even if that place of support you start with is a religious community you're a part of, a networking group, or an online organization. Start somewhere. Don't try to do this moving thing alone.

Need Help Asking for Help?

An example of reaching out when you're feeling like you need support can look similar to expressing openly. Saying something such as *Hey, I'm really feeling stuck and frustrated that I don't feel more settled in yet. I feel silly, actually. Can we talk so I can share some of what I'm going through, and maybe you can tell me I'm normal?*

Or

I'm feeling pretty overwhelmed with all this paperwork I need to do for my new IDs and banking information. Would you sit with me while I go through it, just to keep me company and look in case I have questions?

Or

Hey, I'm really tired. Can you help me carry this?

The trick here is asking for help before you get to burn out. For me, if I wait too long to ask for help, my asking comes out in a tone as if I'm completely resenting the person I'm asking. They can sense the *Why didn't you offer to help me sooner? Iamsoirritatedbyeverything!* tone under my ask. Try it. Just one little thing today, even if you're nowhere near burning out or frustration. There is help available to you somewhere, whether you live alone and that help is online, or grocery delivery, or canceling plans.

On Hiring Help

Sometimes when you think about making your life easier, hiring help can mean hiring domestic help, like someone to come clean your home for you. That's a great resource to use, but not the type of help we're talking about here. I'm talking about emotional support from someone you pay. A counselor, therapist, or life coaches who specializes in anxiety, transition, or supporting people who have relocated. There are also more affordable options through online therapy organizations that allow for text messaging, voice notes, and video call support with sessions covering any aspect of your life you'd like to discuss. Religious leaders you trust can also work here. Hiring support does not immediately banish all difficult emotions, but it gives you more understanding around why they come up and how to work with them in healthy ways. I decided to seek out a counselor in Dubai who was familiar with helping expats adjust. Hiring help gives you a place to go where you know someone is responsible for responding and giving you support, instead of unloading on other family or friends who may want to help, but might not always be best placed to do so.

A note: If you feel uncomfortable with someone you're working with, you have every right to stop and to find someone new. Look for proof of work and, where possible, ask for referrals from people you trust or to speak with someone the coach has worked with in the past. There are many amazing practitioners in the world, and there are occasionally some bad ones. Trust your gut. The right person will challenge you to see things from a new perspective, which might be uncomfortable, but they will never make you believe that you can't survive without them and their help. You should always feel that they are respectful, acting within your best interest, and helping you move forward. Again, if anyone ever tells you that their method is the only way to heal or you feel they're asking you to suppress your heart and gut, they are probably not the person for you.

If working with someone in that way doesn't feel right at this stage, that's okay too. Reach out to places where other people are who have gone through similar experiences. Take advice from people who are living the kind of life you want.

Be Honest and Communicate Your Joys Too

As you settle in more and more, you'll have some really good moments. Lots of them, actually. It's okay to start to enjoy where you are and share all the beauty when it begins to come together. It's totally possible that you get to a place where you feel like your life is better than it's ever been. And then you might start to feel guilty about it. There are people who have way less than you or who are suffering. There is danger and tragedy in the world. Your family may not be able to afford to travel or visit.

Be an example of what's possible anyway. For your family, friends, and the people watching you. For your children or nieces and nephews who observe you. It's okay to be happy too. When you start embracing your feelings, being honest with where you're at, and communicating accordingly, you feel more at home in who you are, and can more happily exist wherever you have landed.

If You Learned Only This

- Being honest with yourself and others about how you feel about your move will help you adjust faster.

- It can be easy to skip over emotional conversations on catch-up calls with friends and family and only stay on the surface. Try to share what's real as often as you can.

- Asking for help doesn't mean you're weak. It means you're smart. Including if you start paying a therapist to help you.

- Be just as honest about your happy moments and joy as you are about the hard stuff. It's not bragging if it's real.

Write It Out

1. How do you really feel about moving right now? Of being away from family and friends? Get it all out. Every last fear, annoyance, relief, and detail.

2. If you feel your mind spinning, answer any of the following questions: What am I really upset about? What do I really want? What am I avoiding? What does my body need? What does my soul need? Where am I just "grinning and bearing it"?

3. What seems so silly to ask for help with, but would actually make life easier, even for five minutes?

4. Who can you ask for that help and when will do it?

Thoughts to Help You

Say Them as Often as You Need.

- Feeling frustrated or sad doesn't mean I'm ungrateful.

- Sometimes I miss my old life. That's okay and normal after such a big change.

- Even though asking for help feels new to me, I'm going to try it anyway. If someone says no, that doesn't mean anything is wrong with me. I can try again.

- I am getting better and better at communicating in ways that feel really satisfying and productive to me.

- My moments of joy are just as important as my sadness. I will pause and savor them.

CHAPTER 8

Taking Care of Yourself

As you begin to settle in further, you may find yourself swinging back and forth from low points to feeling good, and back again. Little things about the new place you live will start to grow on you and even feel endearing, perhaps like the way you are becoming more accustomed to understanding English with varying styles and accents, or relating to jokes about the weather and other things that locals chat about. The unfamiliar will be more familiar.

For me, oddly enough, this Thriving stage began as we got closer to our first visit back to North America for Christmas. We'd missed celebrating Thanksgiving with my husband and family here in Dubai, so as December came closer, I was determined not to make that mistake again. I drove myself forty minutes to the nearest IKEA and bought a starter Christmas tree. It was probably the smallest Christmas tree I'd ever had, but we decorated it together as family. My husband, his mother, his brother, and I, along with our puppy, pulled apart the branches, bending them left and right to fill the spaces, hanging ornaments and twisting the lights around. It was the first time I had decided to be in charge of incorporating a new tradition in our new home. And even though there would never be any actual snow, the coziness of home was present both in our actual home, and in my heart.

I was nervous about the trip back to my family. How would I

feel? Would I see everyone and feel the urge to stay? How would I explain why I hadn't been working at all? I wanted to be confident in my storytelling and didn't want to come across as unsure of myself, which would indicate that I was, in fact, unsure of myself. I was nervous that those feelings might show through and I'd have to confront them. This is where practicing being honest came into play. Buffalo was my birth home—and there were so many things I now loved about it. And it was also not the place where my life currently was. So when we actually arrived back in North America, I was surprised to realize that though I missed the place, I didn't actually want to stay. I was relieved. I recognized there was still more for me to do and experience on the adventure I'd said a whole-hearted yes to just months before. This was my first glimpse of knowing that I was beginning to settle in in Dubai. A couple of weeks into our visit, my husband and I were both itching to get back!

Not So Fast. . . .

And then there was a hiccup. My father and his partner flew back to Dubai with us after Christmas to come see our little corner of the world. We had a really wonderful time. It was a quick weeklong trip, but it felt so nice to finally show people around and see that I did know some things about Dubai now. They were able to see that I was safe, happy, and at home. I didn't want the time to end. It was harder than I expected to say goodbye to them at the airport. Even harder than it was when I left for Dubai in the first place.

As soon as we said our goodbyes, it was as if I was catapulted back to my irritable, resentful, frustrated stage. I felt as though I completely regressed. The footing I thought I found before we left for Christmas wasn't solid and I was back to wondering what my purpose was, what I was meant to build in the world, and if

I really belonged in the Middle East. Being away was hard, but I didn't want to give up.

This time I knew I had to get even more serious about taking care of myself, asking for help, and making it no one else's responsibility but my own to begin to find my way. There was no number of outings that my husband could plan or days spent journaling I could take that would help me fit in more. I had to make meaningful relationships with other women and I had to find something meaningful to spend my time on. Fast. At first, I didn't know where to start, so I turned to social media as I had all of the other times I moved. My first tasks? To schedule coffee dates, find a place to go and exercise, and get clear on the mark I wanted to leave while I was here—all while keeping my One Thing in mind. These new tasks felt exciting now instead of overwhelming.

This stage of the journey is the time when we begin to look toward the future again in the ways that we did when we first made the choice to move, and when we first arrived. We're beginning to come out of our merely existing mentality and we begin to understand why we had to feel so uncomfortable and alone to progress.

One day without realizing it, you'll notice that you step into your new home with real familiarity. You find yourself giving someone else directions to a local restaurant. You tell people that you feel like you're actually enjoying it here now, feeling more like yourself. Give yourself credit—you made it through the hardest part! You've remembered that there is much to look forward to and you hope and faith have returned.

Finding Home Within Yourself

Finding home within yourself means working with both your mind and heart. Bringing them together to play on the same team. Your heart was excited to make the journey, and your mind got scared to keep you safe.

Only you know what works best for you to reach these states. You get to decide. Together in this chapter we'll walk through some of the ways you can create reconnection. Take what works for you and leave the rest. Write your own rules. You moved this far, and only you know what makes you feel free.

I'm not going to tell you to make sure you get up earlier in the morning and meditate. I'm not going to tell you to exercise at least twenty minutes a day or make sure to spend time in nature. I'm not going to tell you to forgive your parents for pain they've caused in your life that's really the root cause of your frustration. All of these things are helpful ideas. But you already know the things you could be doing for yourself that you're not doing. You already know that eating more vegetables is better for your body when you order nothing but carbs and candy bars. You're probably making yourself feel bad enough about "messing up your self care" as it is. I don't mind if you miss a week of work and stayed in bed instead. It's more important that you understand within yourself why you're not doing the things you know are good for you. Sometimes it really is because we just need a break and we feel terrible. Other times it's because we're afraid of what we might accomplish and what people might think if we became the complete best version of ourselves.

The truth is, sometimes I catch the moments of disconnection and take the time I need for myself before physical exhaustion, sickness, or stress kicks in. But sometimes I don't. You may not catch all the storms. But it's better to have the reinforcement beams installed than to have to completely rebuild after the storm passes. And that's what your personal reinforcements are for.

Deep breath. God's got you.
You've got you.

—

The following are specific things I do consistently when I need to reconnect to my heart. Let's dive in.

Learning to Spend Time Alone

I'm grateful I learned the art of going to a movie by myself in late 2016. I watched a Korean drama with English subtitles at the theatre in the middle of Dundas Square in Toronto. I can't remember the name of the film, but it was cheesy and ripe with love story. I got to cry at the cliché parts and spent no energy wondering if anyone would notice. Sometimes, you just have to go to movies you want to see but nobody else does! I like to do experiments like this sometimes, challenging my comfort zone to see if I'll survive. I always do.

But a movie is private, and the theatre is dark. It's not such a hard thing to do. So later that month as part of my "dating myself" experiments, I went to a café in downtown Toronto with a coloring book and colored pencils in my bag. As I sat down next to a table of four women in their early twenties, I thought, *Oh no. They're going to look and whisper about how weird I am.* This was a real test of my confidence. Would I do it? Would I pull out the coloring book and color, as if they weren't sitting a foot away from me? And what was it about being a young woman that triggered all the memories of wanting to fit in as a teenage girl? They were strangers!

I ordered my tea and a chocolate cake slice because if I was going to embarrass myself, at least I was to do it looking like I have good taste in dessert. Minutes went by. I stared at my phone, scrolling at nothing as if that was more acceptable than doing the thing I actually wanted to do. Finally, getting sick of myself, I reached into my bag, flipped through the pages of Millie Marotta's *Animal Kingdom* coloring book, and landed on a picture of an elephant. I wanted to color a snake, but let's not push it. If they looked over, at least a colorful elephant was cool. My hearing was acutely tuned in the women's direction, waiting to hear the scorn I knew would come. And then I heard it. "I wish I could go out on my own like that and color or read," one of the girls said. "I know, right?" her friend replied. And then they went on with their photos of their own magical desserts.

In that moment, something clicked. Sure, some people might think you're weird for doing things blatantly for yourself. But you also never know who you're helping. From that day forward, I've loved going out on my own to sit, watch movies, eat, read, or explore. Those are the times when my mind slows down the most and I see things I've never seen before. When you're going through something that's emotionally difficult, so often the advice we hear is to distract ourselves. "Just keep yourself busy," people would tell me. "Don't let yourself spend too much time alone or you'll go crazy." But for me, it's in the avoiding my own mind that my mind takes over the most. Doing something my heart wants, like trying to be my own best friend, helps to quiet the chatter.

Stop Trying to Do It All

The first thing that's important to remember as you recon-nect with yourself is that your worthiness and value do not come from your level of productivity. Your worthiness and value do not come from doing everything on your own. You are not a bet-ter human being the faster you get "back to normal" after your move. There are so many ways to do things in the world, and if you're blessed with the opportunity to move abroad or travel, you will learn this firsthand. Some of the happiest people have the simplest lives. Many of them went through seasons of life that were quite painful and took a while to get through, just like you have. But somehow, they keep faith, trust, and light in their lives. Why define ourselves by how busy we are? Why force things to happen because you think you should be doing them the way other people do them?

For many years, my life was full of the American Dream par-adox. Like most lower middle class American children, I quickly learned that living costs money and started working as soon as I was old enough. I believed I had to work hard to get things and if I just kept at it, I could succeed. It would take sacrificing friends or family time and delaying happiness to receive happiness in the future. Carrying two to three jobs during university while also being part of extracurricular activities and having no free time was a badge of honor. I was working hard, and the success was coming in the form of job offers. Yet I was still pretty miserable inside, and magically had no money left over after all of the time put in. I had never done the mental and internal work it takes to thrive. I was only doing what I thought I was supposed to be do-ing in the form of action.

Dismantling this cycle takes time, but when I moved to Dubai I was still in a bit in denial that anything about my productivity was different or that I should be any different. I wanted to get right back into things—finding new clients, getting to my health routine, eating better, networking and making new friends so my business could grow, having a stellar relationship with my new husband. As I mentioned earlier, at one point I was determined to find a job because I couldn't take the pace of slowness. I couldn't be still. My mental back-and-forth created physical exhaustion. Could I really keep on going this way, constantly trying to distract myself with Netflix and then feeling guilty about how I could have been working instead?

Your life is still successful if you do less. What you have to prove to other people is nothing. What you have to prove to yourself is that you feel you have given your all to the things that mattered to you. A good question to ask yourself when you're debating whether or not to do something is *Will I regret doing this/not doing this later?* Will I really get anything out of going to a networking event with a speaker panel format and a huge room of people? I might, but using that time to sleep or to reach out to people already within my community and see how they're doing is way more valuable.

When You Want to Share Your Journey Online

Many people who make big moves like this decide to start sharing their stories through blogs and social media as way to connect to themselves, share with other people, and to log their journeys and travels. Many of us also decide to share because it ties into some form of business helping others going through the same. It's powerful to come together and share. I had no idea just how many expat storytellers and expat life coaches there were until I began to write and share my story as well!

Expressing ourselves online and letting our stories be seen can be an extremely fun and encouraging place. Should you decide to take this on, make the decision right now that it gets to be easy. That you can shut off your phone whenever you want to or miss a day or months of sharing and it's still okay. Make the decision that you will use the internet and social media as a tool to help you connect with others, and that the people you connect with will be loving and share in your mission. Promise yourself that when you get tired of it, you will take a break. If you find yourself noticing that you're checking to see how many people have responded or interacted with your posts, picking your phone up right after you set it down—then stop. Stop for an hour, an evening, or a weekend. Re-center. And forgive yourself when you spend an hour or more scrolling mindlessly and pick back up the next day.

A quick note on "authenticity" online: Obviously what you decide is private is also completely up to you. You can choose to share some part of your story and leave your children completely off your Instagram account even though all the other expat mommies seem to be sharing. You can bare it all, or never tell people about your problem with your digestion and acne struggles. It's up to you. You don't have to bear it all to be authentic. If you have something you're feeling emotional about, give yourself the space to work with it on your own first and post when you feel ready.

Amber Rae, artist and author of *Choose Wonder Over Worry*, shared a great quick reference for this on her Instagram account, prompting you to ask before you post: "Why am I posting? Is it for likes & attention? Is it because of a feeling of 'I need to keep up?' Or because 'I have something to say'?"

This is a beautiful way to gage if our social media use is helpful for us. In the image and caption of her post, Amber expands further. If you have something to say—go for it! Share your post.

If you're feeling like you want attention, go and give yourself some love and attention. Offline. And if you feel like you need to keep up, reconnect with your why—the reason behind why you are doing what you do. Connect to the other adventurers you believe you're helping when you share. Connect to your One Thing.

How Good Can You Take It?

You may have heard before that living in the present moment changes everything. The annoying thing about clichés is that people walking around touting them usually have a point. We don't understand it until we feel it or encounter something in our experience that forces us to learn. But close your eyes for a minute and imagine really savoring something. Imagine the pleasure of savouring a food you love—chocolate cake, a delicious tea, or even a really high-end cut of meat, if that's your thing. Those moments you close your eyes and raise your face up to soak in the sun, or watch a live music performance and feel a chill run over your body. Those are the moments that we feel pleasure in our cells. They are natural occurrences that happen all throughout the day. Sometimes we notice them and sometimes they pass us by when they're straight in front of our face.

But this time, as you're wading through the waves of emotions and the randomness of your days in a new environment, you need to create the moments, starting with the things you do every day. Repetitively. How fun can you make showering, brushing your teeth, or washing the dishes? How curious can you get about who invented the toothbrush and what they must have been thinking, or how people went through their lives without showering for days and days? How cool is it that all these things around you exist—even if the only soap you could find at the market is some scent you've never heard of and you're not sure how healthy the ingredients are? When you're cutting fruit for yourself or your spouse or children, can you talk to the strawberry and tell it how you're so glad to meet it, or do you mindlessly chew?

Don't worry about how weird you might seem or feel at first. When we lose the awe factor of our new home, we must be reminded of the awe factors of life itself. Talk to yourself out loud if you have to. There is no one watching but you and God and, personally, I believe God is relieved when I remember how awesome the little things are and doesn't mind my talking. If that's still too much for you, no hard feelings. Try saying thank you to everything you pick up and use in a day. Genuinely look at your water bottle and the water inside and say thank you. Your GPS that helps you find the new market you need to go to? Say thank you. Just for a day, say thank you to everything you touch and see what happens. Experiment with how you interact with life.

Tourist for a Day

Have you noticed how when we're you're on vacation your energy changes? Everything feels a bit lighter as life and work are on hold for a little while. You don't want to leave, and you want to plan your next trip right away. You're more willing to talk to strangers because you'll never see them again, and you want to see and do as much as you can—unless you just want to sit at the beach. What you do is completely up to you, and that's the beauty of it!

When you're in your new home, and especially if you're in the stages where frustration or anxiety are strong, challenge yourself to step into this vacation mindset and energy now and again. Even if you're five years into your settling and you've gotten comfortable in your routine of the places you shop, eat, and walk around, schedule at least one day per month, or a weekend every few months, where you go around your hometown or home country like a tourist. Hire a guide, take lots of pictures, be *that* person who asks a million questions and has no idea what they're doing. Risk looking stupid or sounding stupid. Discover ways to get yourself into vacation mentality even as you step out of the door to your home. Finding ways to remain curious is a great way to reconnect with yourself and experience living. It's what we're here to do!

Sweet Freedom—or Transportation

Unless you're in a major city where you can walk everywhere and public transportation runs twenty-four hours a day, if it's safe and feasible for you, get a car. Relying on public transportation is great and helpful, but having access to a car changed the way I felt about myself. I felt more independent. Less dependent on taxis when I didn't even know how to get around—and at the mercy of their driving. I didn't have to ask my husband to take me somewhere when I just wanted to go sit at a café or the beach on my own. Having that transportation helped me to learn my way around and get used to the many driving styles you'll encounter when you live in a major city with drivers from all over the world.

When a friend of mine, Alexandra, moved from Toronto to Miami in the US, she shared a similar sentiment on her blog: "You need to have freedom to get around. If there's no real public transportation in the city (*ahem*, Miami), you need a car/motorcycle/bike/scooter/whatever. No excuses. Walk, run, fly to the dealership. I was an Uber junkie for the first year I lived here, and I felt like a tourist. Being mobile is the easiest way to feel local."

I concur. You may even be able to test out getting around on your own by taking part in a ride-share or a rental car on days that would be really helpful before you commit fully to a vehicle. Whatever you do, enjoy the sweet freedom of wheels like a teenager again.

Find Something that Smells Good

Flowers, food, candles, essential oils, coffee, even the smell of grass being cut or laundry detergent. In the Middle East, we discovered oud, or scented oils, and you can often find things like incense or candles at the local market. Surround yourself with things that smell good as often and for as long as you can. It's even better if you find a scent that's new to you but loved by the locals. Use your senses to bring you back into the moment and connect with where you are in some way. There's so much goodness for you here. Simple, yet effective.

Make Crying Cool Again

Another great way to reconnect with yourself—which often happens after we finally get honest with ourselves—is crying. Crying is awesome. I think we should do it often and I hope one day it's more normalized. I never used to cry. There was a period in my life where I went through a lot of heartbreak from people I love passing away, first loves ending, and life in general. In that time, I took on that "grin and bear it" persona and prided myself on the fact that I hadn't cried in at least a year. I was a tough cookie, "so mature" and "so strong" after having gone through so much, as those around me liked to say. Inside, I thought that they didn't know the half of what I'd gone through. But what I didn't realize was that by not crying when I was sad, I was also missing out on crying when I felt joy. Nothing moved me. Effectively, I was numb. As I started digging and releasing some of those old experiences, tears started to come more and more—and mostly in happy times! When I felt gratitude, or joy, or love. I could feel more of my emotional spectrum by not being ashamed of this simple bodily function. Almost every day now, my husband will laugh and ask me if I have hit my daily cry quota yet. I'm that good.

Did you know that tears that come as a result of joy, anger, or grief contain more hormones that act as natural painkillers than tears that come, say, because you're cutting an onion? Honestly, our body knows what it's doing! Don't deny yourself some natural medicine. Crying is a release. It's a cleansing. It's an acknowledgment that we are healing something or realizing something about ourselves and the people around us. When we're happy, crying is like a wink from the universe saying, *Yeah, it's pretty great, huh?*

If you feel like you've been holding in emotions, grabbing that journal again is a great place to start. You don't have to write yourself to tears, but just keep writing and write directly to and about whatever feeling you're experiencing. Mention where you feel it in your body—often that place right in the center of your chest. Ask it what it wants. Be angry on the page if you have to. And if you feel an urge to release, cry.

Create a List of All the Things You've Accomplished

Even all the seemingly insignificant things. Track the fact that you brushed your teeth and your hair. If you showered. That you got dressed. That you ate a salad today instead of that takeout you've been ordering. Mark the first day you go to the market on your own or you drive somewhere by yourself. Commemorate your first happy conversation with someone new you've met or your first successful internet connection and Skype call to your family. All these things matter. Everything you're doing every day matters. Celebrate yourself in any moment you can.

Going to my first networking event was a big deal on my list. I put myself out there! Driving to the petrol station and filling up our car was like a grand adventure. Finding all the ingredients I needed for a recipe created a kind of joy that seemed silly at the time but made me remember that making your way in a new place is pretty awesome. Every day, or at least at the end of every week, make a list. You're doing way more than you think you are, and you've accomplished enough that would impress other people. Let it impress you.

Go to Places that Even Remotely Feel Like Home

Oftentimes, there are places that feel familiar wherever you are in the world—or at least remind you of home. Shopping malls, movie theatres, chain restaurants, Starbucks, or even a local bookstore or library can be reminiscent of old creature comforts. Finding these places is a great place to start when you're in a new city. Even if you hate Starbucks. However, you may have moved to a remote place with no creature comforts. In these places, go outside. Go outside at night. Try to find the moon. Stand in awe, when and where you can. These unfamiliar places will start to feel familiar when we connect to the essence of how the planet is a universal home. Should you ever leave this new home one day, there will be memories from it you will ache for. Remember that, and take them in while you can.

These Are All Starting Points

The remaining things you can do to reconnect with yourself and take care of yourself are all the things you know you should do. To-do list items like drink water, move your body, try to learn the new language, go out and try local food, try not to spend too much time on social media, but at the same time reach out to make friends with people on Facebook or Instagram. You can get a new haircut, take a bath, get a manicure, and read more self-help books like this one.

But most importantly, if you only did one thing through this whole journey: give yourself a break. Each of the suggestions in this chapter will help solidify your transition from the Identity Formation to the Thriving stage. When you've started not just accepting but appreciating and being thankful for your reality, something will open up for you. No matter what you've decided to work on or work toward for your life—parenting, building a business, sharing your journey on a blog or social media, recommitting to your studies or a yoga practice. You will find the joys in exploring your new home and your new life. That spark will return. This is the magic of a new place. It will surprise you with how you've learned to love it and the ways you've grown. The thing is, this is true of anywhere we will live. Just like there will always be opposing viewpoints on any topic you can search on the internet, there will always be things you could find to dislike or love about your home. Hopefully, though, the positive adventures of your new life have taught you more about yourself than you will have ever discovered staying put.

If You Learned Only This

- It's possible to feel both good and bad in the same day, in the same hour, in the same breath. Take time for yourself, even for two minutes alone in the bathroom, breathing calmly and remembering you are safe.

- Talk to someone you trust, not to fix anything, but to be heard. Let them in on what you've been feeling and declare, "I just need you to tell me there's nothing wrong with me. That's really what I need to hear right now." (Or ask for whatever it is you need to hear in the moment.)

- Create rituals for the most basic things you do. Laundry, dishes, even brushing your teeth. They will reconnect you to the moment.

- Cry.

Write It Out

1. How do I currently feel about my transition and how I'm doing? Where has there been progress? Where do I still feel lost?

2. How have I been trying to hold it all together? To be super productive? Do I need to continue this?

3. What are the things I used to do before that helped me feel better? Have I been doing them here?

4. Are there any new things I want to try out in order to take care of myself?

Thoughts to Help You

Say Them as Often as You Need.

- Maybe I'll just go for a walk.

- I'm glad I know what I can do for myself to feel better when I need it.

- I am doing really well for myself.

- There's support out there for me when I want it. I only have to ask.

- I'm really enjoying learning how to be happy with my own company.

What a fool
I was to believe
the only one
craving life
was me.

CHAPTER 9

Creating Your Community

Once I was firmly in the Thriving portion of this adventure and I started taking care of myself more, two things became very clear. I really wanted to finally write a book, and I really wanted to test out a theory that there were other women in Dubai like me who wanted to create real, genuine friendships. I wished that when I arrived there was an obvious place to go where other women wanted to talk about things that mattered and preferred cozy tea than going out clubbing. I wished there was an organization that created a simple way to start conversations and make friends as new arrivals in the city—not just places with traditional networking setups or exclusive invite-only memberships.

"I feel like almost all my friendships from back home are changing and we're losing touch. Now I have to make new friends and eventually one of us is going to move and then it's going to suck all over again. Do I really have to do this?" I sat exasperated in the car with my husband on day. We had just realized many of our friends wouldn't be able to fly in for our wedding celebration later in the year.

My husband and I got married in a court ceremony in Buffalo and threw a little going-away party. But we saved the traditional party that included international friends and guests for almost ten months after I moved to Dubai. After getting several declines, my mind wanted to tell me that I was a terrible friend, not connecting with the people I cared about enough. If I had made more of an effort, would they have made more of an effort to be at our "second" wedding?

This disappointment translated to worrying about new friendships in Dubai. Would it be a waste of time to try to make friends and should I just focus on myself and my husband and eventually our growing family? The thought of making new friends and losing them again was tiring.

I felt exhausted and frustrated by it all because I was hurt, and I was trying to protect myself. Of course I still truly desired beautiful and meaningful friendships. Making friends and building community for me isn't a simple want. It's a need, and something I'd only need more if our family grew. Was the community I developed while I was in Toronto a waste of time now that I wasn't living there? Absolutely not. There's no reason not to go all in wherever our feet are planted. My fear was trying to get the best of me.

We Can't Do It Alone

But what is community, actually? And what does it mean for someone whose roots have been dug up and transferred to new soil, or in my case, new sweet sand? In Webster's Dictionary terms, a community has been a group of people who live in the same area or have something in common. This holds true and is a very relevant aspect of community on a sociological level. Today the use of community has expanded into marketing, describing an organization's customer base, event attendees, or even social media followers. It creates a sense of belonging and feeling that those in charge of the community care about the people inside.

But on a personal level, community is those closest to us—those we choose as the village that supports us.

True community is not a place you go to belong and always be agreed with or understood. It's a place where being yourself is the only requirement for being listened to and supported. Where you are challenged to grow and expand. As much as we can create a home within ourselves, our personality, thoughts, and feelings want to be seen by other people. This desire is an innate part of being human and should be embraced. It is in those safe places where we can be witnessed that we start truly trusting who we are. This can't happen if we're only ever in our own company.

Our innate desire for connectedness must be listened to when you are in any kind of transition in your life. And especially when you are placed in a new physical location, with no one familiar around you and a whole new way of living life. When we're in the presence of people who respect us, who are kind, and can relate to something we've gone through, we solidify that confidence in our definition of happiness. Knowing that no matter what happens, we will be able to come back to our center. Our community is a part of that support and re-grounding.

When you move away from home, where the people you're used to reaching out to are not within a quick drive's distance away. . .

When time zones interfere with your schedules and you are figuring out how to talk to the people you love when you're not sleeping, they're not sleeping, and none of you are at work . . .

When you arrive to a new place with nothing but your suitcases (or your significant other) and you're going through all these emotions about settling in . . .

How are you going to find the energy to make new friends or join community organizations? What if you're not sure how long you're staying in your new home anyway?

Begin Where You Are

The best way to build your community is to go deeper with the community you already have. Your family, friends, colleagues, or network. This is true even if you never move in your life. We can always go deeper where we are. Who are the people in your life that you're closest to? Are there things you've been leaving them out of the loop on? Are there desires you have for the relationship to grow? Would you prefer that you stay in contact in a different way or more often? How about that person you ran into and you gave each other the *We have to catch up!* story? Now is your chance to bring these desires to light and to make requests.

It's never too late to reach out to someone if you show them a little bit of kindness and express what you're looking for in a connection with them now. A simple conversation starter could be saying something like, *Hey, you know I've moved and there's been a lot of adjusting! I was thinking of you and realized I'd love it if we stayed in touch more often. Can we figure out a solution?*

If you're feeling especially clear on what you want, ask for a specific schedule. It doesn't have to end up that way, but it gives the person you're sharing with a chance to say what would work for them as well.

What you ask for from your current community depends on what you've decided you want from each relationship. Sometimes you need someone to listen and not give advice. Sometimes you need a friend to come over and help you fold the laundry (or keep you company while you do it, because nobody folds towels like you do). It could be saying to a Facebook friend, *I've been watching you share how you've been getting back into dancing, it's inspiring! I'd love to connect more and hear more about it; I'm trying to get back into dancing too.*

I used to believe that people might think I was a loser if I admitted to not having enough friends around me. But you know what? The people who will be open and cool with your messages will be responsive because you're genuine about it. Don't reach out to people for the sake of hitting a friend quota. Reach out because you think there's commonality. If someone you reach out to isn't into it or doesn't respond, at least you know upfront! You're an adult now, and you get to ask for these things when you desire them. In his bestselling book *How to Win Friends and Influence People*, Dale Carnegie explained that we can make more friends in a few months by being genuinely interested in others than one can in a few years of trying to make others be interested in ourselves. When you mean it in your heart when you ask *How are you doing?* your whole world will change.

No, Really, Who Do You Already Know?

Let's say your relationships with the people closest to you are as close as you'd like them to be. I have another challenge for you. Who are the people you're already acquainted with that you'd like to get to know more?

My move to Dubai prompted a new desire to better get to know more of my extended family. Of course, the news of getting married and moving "to another world" had made its way through the family grapevine. And marrying my husband and introducing him at our going away party and Christmastime also made me realize there are things about my aunts, uncles, and cousins I had no idea about! As soon as you introduce a new person into the mix, they ask questions and start conversations that have never happened before. Which leads to stories and connections that weren't possible before either.

I'm the oldest of sixteen grandchildren on my mother's side of my family. With over a decade between myself and the youngest grandkid, our time together growing up involved me looking over the babies until everyone was at that awkward stage where

I hung out with the adults in a separate room. But now that time has gone by, and cousins are reaching their teens and twenties. We have more to talk about and connect on again. Moving and saying goodbye to them revived a desire to reach out and get to know them in their own way, for who they are as young and not-so-young adults. This is, of course, a work in progress and will be forever, but I couldn't believe that I was in some ways blowing off this huge community I had right in front of me.

These were people with whom I shared relatable experiences thanks to the fact that our parents were raised in the same house. Fifteen other humans with heartbreak and celebrations and ideas that I didn't and still don't know all that much about. I have gone through so much that they don't know about. Would we want to go through our whole lives and realize that we ignored the deepest parts of each other? I don't want to look back and think I took some of my built-in support system for granted. So this is an area I am working on.

What's the harm in getting to know that family member who's always intrigued you, or the one you've heard stories about but never firsthand? If it's "not the way our family does things," then I challenge you to ask yourself if you want to continue that legacy or create one that feels good for you.

But if you find yourself thinking that there's no one in your life you could go deeper with, this has to be false. I know of course there are people we don't want to get closer to because of trauma or unhealthy relationship patterns. That is fair. But there are often relationships in my own life that have gone uncared for because of small things I was uncomfortable bringing up. Feelings about making an effort to stay in touch were never addressed, and that can cause months of disconnection. This can happen because of pride, hoping they'll reach out first, and even because we tell ourselves we're too busy to deal with it right now. Being too busy to deal with a relationship that was once important to us can be a sneaky way our egos try to avoid confrontation or prove we are "right"—when really, we're hurt.

If there are any people in your life with whom you could connect more deeply, you've likely already thought of them by reading this chapter. Get clear on what you desire for yourself and with those people and take a risk and reach out to them. If for no reason at all other than to show yourself you can take a risk, fail, and survive. But in a lot of cases, you'll create a stronger relationship because of it.

Making New Friends

Many of us have enough people in our lives that we could spend all our time just going deeper with them. But moving to a new place is also about the fun of new connections! So focus on one or two current connections to start, and work on new ones consistently overtime. In fact, work on whatever feels good to you. Because new friends can also be some of the best friends you've ever had. But before you run out into your new world or search online for your new best friend, it's important to ask yourself what you even want to get out of new friendships and community.

It's easy to hop online and search for "expat community" or "yoga community," but neither of those things really tell you who the members of those communities are, other than that they are foreigners and do yoga. That doesn't mean you'll click. The first time I logged onto one of the major online communities for expats, I felt no soul in it. Sure, I could join a walking group or an international cuisine meetup, but what kind of people would be there? I tried reaching out to a couple of women I saw there who expressed interest in wellness and chatting over coffee, but didn't get any responses. I've also attended women-in-business events, another one of my interests, but found that if there was a speaker and I was there by myself, it was more difficult to walk right up to a group of women and insert myself into the conversation.

That's when I knew I had to switch up my strategies. Now, this was all happening when I was still bouncing in between the Identity Formation and Thriving stages of my transition. That's when I remembered I had to connect myself not to who I was in that moment, but to the woman I wanted to become. Did that woman hang around the same kinds of people she hung out with in Toronto? Was she surrounded by anyone new and different? Were there any changes in her life that meant her interests also changed? Of course. I had gotten married, stopped drinking alcohol, moved a few thousand miles away, and also wanted to focus on my health and work. The differences were major.

In Toronto I was single, still drinking, working as a copywriter, and more focused on my mental and emotional health than my physical health. I have amazing friends in Toronto, and as I reflected, I realized that many of them were like the me I was then. Our conversations revolved around our budding businesses and our personal development. They were relationships that were so needed at the time. Now there was room for new kinds of friendships that would be supportive for me as I stepped into my life here.

For example, I realized that I'd like to shift from only finding examples of the women I wanted to be in news articles and biographies, and instead making a friend like that in real life! A woman who is navigating a marriage, has experienced raising young children, and who is running a business she loves. Since a lot of my friends were my age, or had some part of that Rachael's Future Marriage/Babies/Business trifecta missing, this showed me an area of friendship I could aspire toward. I desired to be around someone I enjoyed speaking with, who had similar values and desires for life, but who also had experiences that made them much wiser than myself.

Luckily for me, what better place in the world than Dubai to find women who were hardworking, kind, good mothers, and had happy relationships? Remember, my definition of happiness does not equal always sunshine and roses. There's always more to the story. But I had my cornerstone desires in hand—friendships with happy, married working moms. Once I was clear the type of friend I wanted, the right women showed up, through following me on Instagram, coming to my events, or introductions from someone else.

As you begin to use your imagination about the life you're building in your new home and the kinds of relationships you want to have, ask yourself:

- What type of person do you want to be?

- What types of friends do you envision that person having?

- What parts of your physical and emotional life do you want to grow and have more support in?

- How do you want to feel when you're in the presence of new friends or in a group?

- When you leave a coffee date or a gathering, what kinds of tools or feelings do you want to come home with?

- Where do those kinds of people hang out?

It doesn't matter if you start by meeting people in your new hometown or over the internet. Make it a goal to meet one new person you can really share your story with. One new person who makes you feel at home, whether in their physical presence or over messages. Give yourself a chance to be seen and to see someone else in return.

Creating Community You Need But Can't Find

One evening, at the first business event for women I went to in Dubai, I heard the statement, "It's really hard to make good friends in Dubai!" In that moment I realized I had a choice. I could choose to believe it was hard and feel defeated, as if one more thing was stacked against me. Or I could choose not to. I decided then and there I wasn't going to let myself walk around with that assumption. I was in Dubai, and this woman was here making that statement in Dubai. So here we are, two people who wanted to make good friends in the same room. What was the problem? Of course, there was basis for accuracy in this woman's statement. In all big expat cities, many people leave or move and then you have to go through the feelings of "losing" a friend all over again. I knew that I had to decide I was going to make real friends even though our locations were guaranteed to change. Does how much we're willing to love change based on how and when the "end" comes? As if we can schedule that into our planners.

Choose to keep your heart open without exception, even when you know it's going to hurt.

—

I wanted to test my theory that there were other women in Dubai who were craving good friends. A few Instagram posts later, and our first Women Connect Abroad gathering at a local teahouse had fourteen women. At the second event a month later, I had to turn women away because the café was full. Some of the attendees said it was the best "networking" event they'd ever been to in their decades living in the city. It was clear that my desire for real friendships and my honesty about why I wanted them was something other women wanted too. There was no reason to push against it or avoid it. But there are, of course, a ton of reasons we tell ourselves we are safer in the comfort of our own homes.

There's a way around some of that fear. If you want to build a community for yourself, get clear on which parts of who you are you'd like to share and how you want to help. Those aspects will draw in the right people. For example, at my first Women Connect Abroad event, I was hesitant to share that I didn't drink. Even though we're in an Islamic country, there's a huge community of expats who decide to drink. My time in New York City conditioned me to believe that brunch and happy hour were the only activities you could partake in besides working. Nobody would want to sit around with me and drink tea, right? But the core reason I started these gatherings was so I could connect with women interested in similar things, and to connect them to each other. So I knew I had to share my full story. I began explicitly writing in the captions of our promotional posts that there'd be no alcohol at events. I declared that we were the opposite of happy hour. I took that opportunity to share a central part of our messaging. Having sobriety be a nonnegotiable part of my life meant that people who didn't like that didn't come in the first place. Instead, many of the women who came privately asked me why I stopped, and how to cut back themselves. Turns out, honesty is the perfect filter for the right friends.

Whatever your personal interests or experiences are, there's no way no one out there can relate to you in some way. If you can't find a community focused around what you're looking for, that means you have an opportunity to create a space where other people finally feel heard. You get to help people by going first. By sharing first. By doing it your way.

It all comes back to remembering how powerful you are. Sharing the parts of your story that you choose to share is a way your power is felt by your community. You can lead them to awareness within themselves. Even if what you're sharing is that you're terrified of not making any good friends in your new home. Your story is where your leadership begins, and the right community will align with you because of it.

Create Space for Sharing

When you've gathered a person or a few people together, the fastest way to help facilitate bonding is to create a shared experience. Creating shared experiences through telling our stories is my ideal way to do this. Storytelling in small groups allows people to connect faster than when you're going to a networking event or business panel where the guests don't mix with each other.

If you start with the intention for this type of connection, the location of your gathering doesn't even matter. If you're inviting people to join you in a gathering at a café, or at the beach, or even in your apartment, create a way for the individuals to share a part of who they are with the group. There are many ways to do this. You can create questions that guests randomly pick out of a bowl to answer. There are decks of cards and books and blogs that give great examples of these. At the first few Women Connect Abroad gatherings, we used a specific deck of cards called *Ask Deep Questions* that was created by a friend of mine, Jan, in Toronto. His deck combines mildly personal questions like, "What does the ideal weekend look like for you?" with deeply personal questions such as, "Who taught you how to love?" In our first gatherings, guests took turns sharing, and everyone loved it. You may choose to focus your questions based on the topic of your meeting or keep them general, like we did to begin. Creating that space is a perfect way to skip the awkward small talk and lead everyone to respectful, loving connections.

Cyndie Spiegel, author of *A Year of Positive Thinking* and one of the first women who hired me in New York City, is a creator of communities herself. Both in online and in person spaces, she's a leader in facilitating events, talks and communities designed to "transform the behavioral status quo of women." Basically, she walks the talk while admitting she's also still figuring things out along the way. I've seen that integrity spill out into her work and communities. One of the foundations of building a community, she believes, is civility. Demonstrating mutual respect. And how do you do that? "It starts with mindful listening," she said in a podcast interview. "I'm not going to cut you off. I'm going to listen to what you have to say. Whether I agree or disagree, I'm going to listen. I'm not going to multitask while you're having a conversation with me. As the leader of these groups and founder of these groups, how I treat the women that are within these groups matters." Your leadership, and how you treat yourself and the individuals who join you, sets the tone for how the community will run and grow.

Yes, it makes a difference even if there's only one person who showed up to your first gathering. You may not have the mental space or calendar space to go all out starting a brand-new company or meetup group. And you don't have to. A community can simply start with two people.

Being Yourself Saves Time

I want to emphasize the importance of knowing the core of who you are and sharing that with the world. When you're new somewhere it's easy to want to make friends—any friends.

The emotional stress and pain we put ourselves through by claiming we're interested in things we're not means we create a false basis for friendship. Eventually, we'll get tired of pretending. Sometimes this is an easy adjustment for the people around us and our friends stick around. Sometimes relationships end when we are more open about who we really are. When you've made a huge move and a transition like this, you have an opportunity to start fresh with new friendships. There is no reason to spend the emotional time creating an image that isn't real. Allow yourself to be even 5 percent more free with who you are than before, and the people you find around you will be the best fits you've ever had.

Trusting Your Gut Around Who You Spend Time With

Being yourself also means you're allowed to be fierce and discerning with who you spend time with. Throughout my moves, I've made the mistake of making plans with new potential friends simply because the image I saw of them looked good to me, even when my gut told me something wasn't working. There have been women I have thought would make the most amazing friends because they are into yoga, spirituality, and wellness, with similar life goals to me. We'd spend time together over coffee or having a girls' night, and I'd wonder why something wasn't quite clicking. I'd try again—one more lunch, one more phone call—yet the feeling would still be there. Other people seem to love this person, so was something wrong with me? My rational mind was trying to override my gut and my body's signals. It's like the dating phrase "they looked good on paper" when a woman thinks that because a man has a good job, he will make a good husband. Sure, he could, but maybe not for you.

If you don't feel energized after spending time with someone, ask yourself why. It's okay to give it another try, but pay attention to what your body is telling you. You are still a good person if you don't want to hang out with someone who seems nice. I'll repeat that. You are still a good person if you don't want to hang out with someone who seems nice. Thou shall not ignore gut feelings.

It's possible that insecurities or comparison will come up as you're meeting people. Especially if there are religious or cultural differences you're learning and you're not sure where you fit. It's also possible that your gut feelings of disliking a person are actually telling you that you're afraid the person is better than you in some way. That fear is possible of men as well, but if you're a woman you know there's nothing quite like comparing ourselves with other women.

This is the complexity of gathering with other women in societies where we're taught to be afraid of there being someone better, more attractive, or more put-together than us. Of being taught that to get ahead, we need to do that while stepping on the shoulders of other women to pass them. For a large part of my life growing up, I didn't believe that more than one woman could be the same level of brightness in a room at the same time. I thought that if someone was shining brighter than me, then there was a reason and I should not interrupt or try to intervene. And we for sure couldn't be friends. Luckily, thanks to so many women brave enough to lead in their own way, this paradigm is changing. We can support each other and collaborate. Even if we're building businesses doing the same things or talking about the same topics. Deep down in our hearts we don't want to compete, but in some of our minds we're afraid of not being good enough.

When we see other women doing things well or what appears to be successfully, it can be a way to make ourselves feel terrible or it can inspire us to see what's possible. Choose to believe that all people can inspire you about something, and that you are just as valuable as they are. But still, always trust your gut.

Yes, but I'm an Introvert

My dear, beautiful introverted friends. You are the best at building community. Tight-knit communities. Because your introvertedness doesn't mean you don't like to connect with people or that you're bad at it. It's a reflection of how you re-energize yourself. And if you're like me, that means you re-energize with some quiet time rather than with large groups of people like our extroverted friends. This all goes back to choosing positive labels for ourselves. If you're telling someone you're an introvert like you believe it's a bad thing, then of course you're going to feel bad about yourself! But who made the determination that introversion or extroversion are good and bad? You decide what you want your life to be like and what definitions of introversion you want to define you.

Being in a community doesn't have to mean that you are leading the community, if that's not what you want. Start connecting with people in ways that feel good for you. Typically, when you're in a new place, that can begin online through social media messages or comments. It can begin by showing up to the same yoga class over and over and finally speaking to the person on the mat next to you. Take a risk to put yourself out there and invite them for coffee or a walk in your new neighborhood. I have said directly to new people that I am looking for friends or that I want to be their friend. There's nothing to be ashamed of when it's the truth! Especially if you decide to join community groups online or over social media. Pop in and say, *Hey, I'm new here!*

Do not be afraid. You will be a little, but that's normal. Fear is a liar that will tell you you'll never make the kinds of friends you want. Everyone who has come to any gathering I've hosted tells me privately that they were nervous before they came. We are all afraid of rejection. Be someone who helps people feel loved, within the boundaries of what you're capable of, and your community will come naturally. You are worthy of being seen. Do not let your introversion make you think you need keep your heart from being witnessed in its glory.

Community is one of the most vulnerable places of our lives. We have to choose to engage with everyone around us openly while also risking that rejection. We need to keep showing up for ourselves and trusting that we will find our place. That place won't be everywhere. It doesn't need to be. Often, we can get so excited about being connected to the "right" people on paper (or social media) that we don't check in that they're the right people for our souls. Whether it's the family we were born into or the family we chose, our communities are multifaceted. No matter the cultural differences, lead with your heart and your truth. You will find the people you're looking for.

If You Learned Only This

- Expand your connections and your reach with the people already in your life—your family, friends, and even people you've always been curious about but never dedicated the time to getting to know.

- A community is where you go to be yourself, be heard, and to listen. It is not a place where everyone always agrees with each other.

- Being yourself from the beginning saves everyone time.

- A community starts with two people. That is enough.

- If you can't find what you need in a community, build one.

- Everyone wants to make good friends, they're just not sure where to start. You go first.

Write It Out

1. Who are the people you already have in your life? How can you reach out and re-connect with them? Do it now.

2. What kinds of friends would you love to have in your life? What are their values and interests? How will they be supportive of you? Journal out your dream BFF or community.

3. Is there a need for a specific type of community in your new area? What would you have loved to know existed when you first moved?

4. What deadline will you give yourself to go to a new event or two? Mark it in your calendar.

Thoughts to Help You

Say Them as Often as You Need.

- This move could be an opportunity to get to know the people I love even more deeply.

- I love getting to know myself more, which makes me want to know and love others.

- Seeing someone else succeed shows me what is possible in my own life.

- I am learning to be comfortable spending time in community.

- Allowing in support and sharing myself with others feels like a relief.

- I trust myself to know where I should be, and who I should be with.

Take it easy.
80 percent of
the pressure you
put on yourself
is unjustified.
—A reminder
from my husband

CHAPTER 10

Visits with Family and Friends

Once you've reached the point where you feel like you're thriving in your new home, the most difficult moments will be the milestones—birthdays and anniversaries, holidays and health problems. Birth of children, new careers, graduations and bridal showers. It's painful to not be physically there with people you love to celebrate and support each other. Truthfully, if I let myself think into the future, the scariest part for me is imaging when someone I love dies. Will I regret the last thing I said to them or not staying in touch the way I wish we did? Will it make me wish I never made this move and I will always regret it? I have read that grief is a response to all the love we feel like we didn't get to share with someone. And because we are infinite, at the core our love is unconditional. That's a lot of love to feel like we're holding in.

But playing into that fear of making a mistake only means we're wasting time not loving the people we're so concerned about missing. When we are happier where we are, the time spent with other people is more joyful, calm, and connected. Essentially, taking care of ourselves is the best way to ensure we are giving our best to those we love in the time we have with them!

Pressure to Do All the Things and Get Everything Right

Throughout the time I spent writing this book, I visited North America three times. I had family come visit us in Dubai three times. I'd venture to guess six visits in our first year abroad would be more than any other year in the future. On each of these trips I'd been excited to go "home" and have quality time as a family. I expected myself to miss each of the people I saw and then pretty much go on with my life. The truth is, visiting or having visitors can bring up a lot of emotions. It can also feel pretty stressful.

Here are some reasons visiting family and friends after you move is hard:

- Feeling pressure to see everyone you miss in one trip.

- Witnessing family's and friends' sadness and grief about you being away and them missing out on your life, and feeling guilty about it.

- Remembering to dress and act more local to home, if there's a difference.

- Visiting places with old (and sometimes not positive) memories, reminding you of who you used to be.

- Talking about when you'll be back next, for how long, and your hypothetical plans.

- Diving headfirst back into family dynamics you haven't been around.

- Learning about changes in people's lives they didn't share with you on catch-up calls because they didn't want you to worry.

- Seeing the inevitable change in people you love because of time.

- Driving near and far to see people because "we were the ones who moved so why should they have to make all the effort?".

All these reasons will never be enough for me to not visit. Visiting is so special. But it's really hard because it forces everyone to be reminded how much they love and miss each other. To hear fear in the back of their minds about what will happen in between visits. But you know what? This is true of everyone's life. As people who live abroad, we are forced to feel these things instead of ignoring them or writing them off.

Through these many visits, after burning out from running around trying to see everyone and maintain balance for my husband and my work, I have a few strategies that have helped.

What's Your One Thing for This Visit?

You've created your One Thing, your guiding light for your life in your new city. But before you leave to go visit your family, try creating one for this specific trip.

Ask yourself *If I only accomplished one satisfying thing on this visit home, what would that be?*

You could be going back to visit for a specific purpose, like a wedding, introducing your baby to family, or visiting someone who's sick. You could be going for a holiday visit or big anniversary. You might be going because it's summer break. Whatever the timing, really focus in on what you hope to get out of this time. Return to it when things start to feel overwhelming.

Unpack Your Suitcase

I'm not sure why it took me so long to figure this out, but on the first couple of trips to my parents', I kept all of my clothes folded in the suitcase, even when we were there for a few weeks! For my husband and I, we move around among different family members' places and hotels, so it seemed easier to just leave it all there. But on my last trip of the year, I finally placed my things in the hotel drawers. I hung up dresses on the hangers and laid my shoes out in a line. It was a simple thing, but the organization felt good. Make your life as simple as you possibly can during this time.

Having a semblance of order with your things means you can spend more time on how you're feeling rather than freaking out when you can't find that shirt you packed at the bottom of the bag.

—

Schedule a Day Off

A couple chapters ago I said I wouldn't tell you to wake up twenty minutes earlier to meditate in your new home. So I won't tell you to do it in your old one. But be aware that any kind of routine you usually have when you're not visiting is going to be seriously challenged. Your days will be so full of people who want to see you and whom you want to see that you may forget to eat, or otherwise look after yourself. On longer visits, do whatever you possibly can to warn anyone you want to be around that you're going to reserve at least one day for yourself. That means no visiting and maybe even no calling or texting. Do something you want to do. Sleep all day. Don't leave the hotel room. If you can't take a day, take five minutes alone in a bathroom and breathe. Seriously. It sounds silly if you haven't been home visiting yet or had guests staying with you for a month (or you don't have kids), but you will cherish this time.

It's Okay to Say No

It's the worst feeling to have plans with someone and then realize you're so tied up or stretched thin that you have to cancel the visit. Even if I've seen my mom or dad ten times in one trip, I get so anxious that if I don't see them that one more time, we'll all be sad. But on my last trip home, the irritation and anger that reminded me of the Acting Fine phase of transition was hitting my husband and me hard. We were bickering over nothing for two days before we realized we had hit our limits. I had a deadline for this book, so we were craving some time alone to work, and time alone with each other watching Netflix. Unfortunately, this meant we had to rearrange our schedules. I met a friend for girl time without him while he slept. I canceled morning breakfast plans to sit in the hotel lobby and write. The more things you have to do, the more nourishment you need to help you reset yourself. Try trading in one of those extra cups of coffee for a canceled dinner date and some sleep.

You'll Miss Your New Home

You may be surprised by how much you want to go back to your new home while you're visiting friends and family. Little things you didn't realize you found endearing will be missing from your culture. Your worldview will change and seeing old family and friends will remind you how lucky you are to see things in a new way. There are new friends and community to miss, events happening there you'll have to skip. Let this catch you off guard. This is the privilege of living this kind of full life.

Return to Your Communication

When you're home, don't forget to continue to be as honest as you can be in all forms of communication. Let people in on how your life is really going, how you miss them, how you'd prefer to stay in touch with them once you leave again. This is hard, and it still is for me when all I want people to know is that I'm okay, happy, and just want them to be happy too. Your ability to communicate directly impacts your connections with people. Try your best. People may not always respond the way we want, but we live with as few regrets of things left unsaid as possible.

Make Some Noise

This is a tip I've utilized any moments where I feel like I'm going to lose it during visits. Stop looking at your phone or spending time on the computer speaking to no one. If you're physically able, stand up and shake your arms, shake one leg at a time (unless you have some special hovering skill), and shake your head. Breathe in through nose and out through your mouth making an audible sound. A sigh, a *haaaaaa* breath, a *sssssssss* sound or even a yell, depending on what you're feeling. Play around with the noises. Shift your body around so that you can move the energy of what you're feeling. Hear your own voice. Speak out loud to yourself. Remember how powerful your voice is, and how your energy shifts when you use different tones. Turn on a song and sing. Notice your vocal cords vibrating. Hum a tune in the shower or as you walk around the house. When you're feeling really adventurous, hum in public. The point here is simply to get out of your head and back into your body. Since you have to breathe thousands of times per day anyway, this is the easiest place to start.

When in Doubt, Lie on the Floor

I'm not sure what it is about falling and sprawling straight out on a hard floor, staring at the ceiling. Maybe it's the solid feeling of being supported with nowhere to fall. But lying on the floor and staring without doing anything relaxes me when I'm most exhausted. It creates a surrendered feeling—a *don't anyone bother me, I'm just going to be here* moment where I laugh at myself in recognition that it looks funny when I just suddenly lie down in the middle of someone's living room. Yogis have of course studied the benefits of this pose but try not to think too much about why it's good for you. Just try it in your hotel room or old bedroom at Mom's house and see if it feels good. You may fall asleep. That's all you need to know.

Don't Forget to Cry

Every visit, I cry saying goodbye to a different person, and people cry whom I didn't expect would. Every visit, I think this will be the one that'll be easier and I won't get sad or wish things were different. That doesn't happen. I won't even say it gets easier. We just get better at it. Through all of this work, we get better at allowing ourselves to go through the feelings. To accept them as normal. So, when you visit someone you love, don't forget to cry if you feel tears coming.

The Journey Is Forever

When I started this book, I shared the phases I would walk you through. I let myself, and you, believe that once you got to the end—Identity Formation and Thriving—that was it. Ongoing, wonderful happiness and success. Actually, the opposite is true. As people who live somewhere away from family and friends, we will continue to have moments we have to say goodbye, feel isolated and alone, doubt our identities, find more community, and feel settled. And then someone leaves, something happens in our family, or we move again and the cycle restarts itself.

Don't forget that the same is true for everyone, even the people who never move away. We all say goodbye to people and things, pretend everything's fine, hit a moment of truth, feel depression and confused about who we are, and hopefully, we return to alignment. That's why, even though this book is technically about feeling at home when you move—it's more about feeling at home with yourself no matter what. When you can embrace transitions and trust yourself with tools to manage them, you will be living the fullness of life.

If You Learned Only This

- Every visit home or to family and friends will feel different and will be hard and lovely in their own ways.

- It's okay to not be able to see everyone, or to take some time for yourself.

- Remember to communicate honestly and let people know how you're really feeling. Just because you're visiting doesn't mean you have to be perfect.

- The transition journey is forever. Life will cause us to be siphoned through the cycles at each new goodbye. You have the tools you need to flow through more gracefully.

Write It Out

1. What is the One Thing you could accomplish during your visit that would make you call the trip a success? Get clear on your One Thing.

2. Before you go for a visit or have someone come, where can you schedule in some alone time? Do that now.

3. Where are you feeling pressured on this trip? Who do you feel you have to see? What family dynamics or current issues is everyone facing that's worrying you?

4. Is there anything you want to make sure you communicate or say?

Thoughts to Help You

Say Them as Often as You Need.

- I am really grateful so many people love me and want to spend time with me.

- Thank you for giving me the chance to visit.

- Communicating from my heart helps me feel heard.

- I am present with the people in front of me.

- It's okay for me to pause and breathe.

*Surrender
to the journey
of life and
you'll be
created anew.*

CHAPTER 11

Celebrating When You Feel at Home

As you've worked your way through this book, there have been ups and downs. Celebrations and setbacks. You will hardly notice the moment you feel more natural in this place you now call home. Going to and from the store, work, or meeting new friends will happen without nervousness or a feeling of *I'm a stranger here*. And when that moment happens, you'll smile to yourself and remember how much dedication you put in to get to this place. All the things you had to go through, feel and learn. You'll know there will always be something new to deal with, another local surprise in store, but you have more confidence to take it on. You'll start to laugh at the same jokes locals make about the weather or how people behave on weekends. Family will come to visit, and you may find yourself thinking, *Hey, I think I really like this, couldn't you all just move here instead?*

Aside from knowing that you can handle anything you need to, my desire is for you to also know it is okay to be happy. It is safe to feel like you're living out your definition of happiness.

My life for so many years carried a tinge of anxiety, waiting for the other shoe to drop. My body was often in fight-or-flight and my nervous system was over-adrenalized. Stress was a habitual state, and I am still calming my body and soul out of this reactive place. So when I was going on almost a year of peace in Dubai, doing work I really enjoyed and making friends whom I loved almost from first sight—I honestly felt like something was about to go really wrong. It couldn't possibly be this good, so I should prepare myself. My mind would find ways to create another thing to worry about. There was no end to this madness in the striving for perfection.

I also thought that because I no longer had the same "problems" to talk about, I'd become unrelatable to the people closest to me. As I mentioned at the start of this book, for a long time so much of my identity was encompassed by a few focal points—my desire to hack "self-love," being single and dating drama, wondering how I would pay my bills and what to do with my life and career.

All of these focuses, in some way, became the main topics of conversation with people around me. My friends and I had the same dating issues, my family and I could relate because we had similar financial histories, and everyone I knew was working on some parts of their career that wasn't fulfilling. Slowly, as I stopped trying to hack self-love and just loved myself (loving yourself is, in its essence, also loving yourself for the times you don't love yourself), as I trusted I would always have enough and life started to reflect that, as I matured when it came to being in relationship, and when I surrendered to my calling as a writer. . . all of those problems I identified myself as having disappeared. And I was afraid—what would we talk about now if we stopped talking about these shared problems? My mind wanted me to sacrifice the beauty based on the threat that I'd lose the people I cared about most because we had "nothing in common anymore." But that fear wasn't true. We had more in common than ever before, because the love has never left.

As You Move Forward

This hasn't been a story about all the tangible things you can do when you move to start to fit in. It's not about the specifics of living in a place with different values, religion, or government. It's not about adhering to local customs or tips for acclimating to a new job. This has been a story of remembering your power and choosing your happiness for yourself. You don't have to be an elected official or even remotely rich to wield this strength. Do whatever it is you need to do to remember this, as often as possible. Your happiness moves with you wherever you go.

Expect to be on your own timeline for feeling like you've settled in. Expect that occasional aches for your family and the places you grew up will never fully go away. For all of history people have immigrated to new places and there's a reason we tend to band together with people who are familiar. The places, families, and cultures we come from provide a sense of meaning for us. Don't expect to lose that connection just because you sleep in a different location.

There are many people who have taken this journey of moving somewhere new and realize they don't like it. There are many people who yearn to go back to their original homes but can't for some reason, or feel like they just made all of this effort to get settled somewhere, and now it's time to go again. Only you can know what's best for you.

Where Is Your Home?

What life can you discover in all of the new homes you have created?

Home with self.
Home with family.

Home with community.
Home with location.

Each facet of home requires its own care and attention. Give to each willingly and feed them. Tend to yourself. Call your family. Invite a new friend for tea. Learn about the place you now live.

⟡

Whatever your beliefs, this planet is our home. Wherever we move to on it, we are home. The places are not separate from us. Its people are not separate from us.

—

Where is your home? How will you interact with the world? Well, that's for you to decide. But I hope you'll return to the tools laid out in these pages and the resources currently available when you're feeling like your home is unsettling or not for you. Return to your One Thing—that outcome or goal that would make you feel so satisfied with your move, even if it's the only thing that happened.

Check in with yourself around your expectations—mostly of yourself, and then of other people. Ask for help and share your story in ways that feel good to you, and only when you want to. Finding grace in these fast-paced moments means listening to your true core and what will really serve you. Sometimes that means speeding up and filling our schedules. Oftentimes, it means slowing down—way more than appears socially acceptable. Your social media followers can wait and will understand. You will come back stronger.

Remember that you are not alone. And you don't have to be perfect to be happy in this crazy big world.

I am with you. And you've got this.

Acknowledgements

My unrelenting gratitude to . . .

My Creator, who has made this life possible. Thank you for always staying with me and by me, even when I forget. Thank you for embracing me when I leave and when I return. Your perfection is seen all around me.

My husband, supporter, and best friend. Every day I look back on our story and I am amazed by how magnificent you are. I am never more myself than when I am with you, because you have seen me all along. Thank you for forgiving me and embracing our future. None of this would have been possible without you. I love you.

Mom—I love you. Thank you for planting the seeds of what is my spiritual life, my open-mindedness, my empathy, and my ability to love. All of that has led me here. I am grateful not only to look just like you, but to be like you.

Dad—as if we could get closer, this journey over the last year of the book I think has done it. Thank you for all of the ways you show me that you want me to be happy, and for loving me with your whole heart. I love you forever.

My family—my grandparents, Aunt Stacey, Aunt Joan, and all the aunts, uncles, and cousins who supported my big leaps even when they were confused or nervous for me. Thank you for loving me and cheering me on.

Thalia—my editorial director. Your guidance and faith has gotten me through the very first major work I have ever followed through on. I'm not sure you understand how big that is. Thank you for your time, suggestions, and beautiful thoughts about life. Here's to more adventures.

Kira and The Dreamwork Collective team—Kira, thank you for your patience and encouragement as I made the decision to take the leap. The work you do in the world sets people free. To Marinda, my copy editor, and Myriam, my designer. Thank you for helping bring this to life.

Anna—your encouragement of me and your faith in me always surprises me. You have calmed me down and corrected me in ways no one else can. Thank you for being there with me. I love you and I miss you always.

Palak—the best thing I ever did in Toronto was say yes to an invitation to Cookbook Club. Thank you for all of your love and support and for growing together.

The Council of Ladies—two very best friends of mine that sustain our connection over calls on the internet. We have been through so much and I'm so grateful to have had you along for the ride. More magic is on its way.

My Women Connect Abroad friends—thank you for having faith in me and for being the reason I started to feel at home.

My coaches and unofficial mentors over the years—Kavita J. Patel, Preston Smiles, Alexi Panos, Amber Rae, Matthew Cooke, Cyndie Spiegel, Amanda Frances, Leroy Milton—thank you for who you are in the world and the work that you do simply by being who you have to be. In big and small ways you have impacted my life and inspired me to surrender to magic.

Amanda Ranae—you have impacted my life and the life of my family. I am inspired by you. Thank you for helping me call myself forward and become a leader.

Myself—thank you for sticking it out with me. I'm here for the ride and I'm so proud of you. I love you.

Notes

Chapter 8: Taking Care of Yourself

Orlando, A (2019, Feb 27). What they don't tell you about moving [Web log post] from www.alexandraorlando.net

Amber Rae [@heyamberrae]. (2019, March 2). Ever ask yourself, "Should I post this?!" Here's a compass. [Instagram Photo]. Retrieved from https://www.instagram.com/p/BvRrtJkha9D/

Chapter 9: Creating Your Community

Domitrz, M. (Producer). (2018, November 28). *The Respect Podcast: Exploring Work. Love, & Life* [Audio podcast]. Retrieved from https://www.mikedomitrz.com/articles/026-cyndie-spiegel-on-online-communities-women-respect/